Touring the
COTSWOLDS

Jim Watson

Lychgate, Bisley

CITY BOOKS • BATH • ENGLAND

A Cotswold doorway

First published 2019

City Books, c/o
Survival Books Limited,
Office 169, 3 Edgar Buildings,
George Street, Bath BA1 2FJ, United Kingdom
Tel: +44 (0)01305-266918
email: info@survivalbooks.net
website: citybooks.co/survivalbooks.net

British Library Cataloguing in Publication Data
A CIP record for this book is available
from the British Library.
ISBN: 978-1-909282-91-9

Contents

Naunton from the B4068

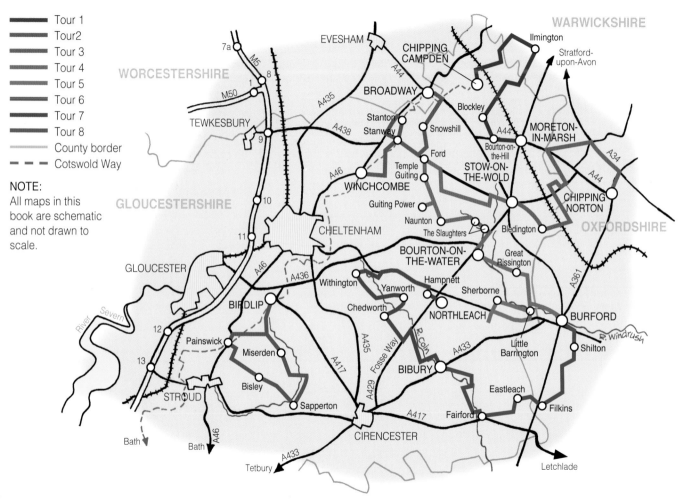

Introduction

The Cotswolds are unique, a timeless landscape of tranquil country lanes, rolling hills and deep wooded valleys. Its small towns and villages are places of warm, honey-coloured stone, steeped in history and with an undefinable 'Englishness' that makes you immediately feel at home. The favourite haunt of royalty and the landed gentry for centuries, and now also of latterday show-biz 'celebrities' and rock stars, the region has no precise boundaries. There are those who argue that it extends as far south as Bath, but for me its essence is concentrated most richly within the county of Gloucestershire.

This book takes you on eight tours of prime Cotswold country, visiting tourist hotspots and secluded villages with ancient churches, while enjoying expansive views of magnificent countryside.

The Cotswolds are also foodie heaven these days, attracting top awards, often for restaurants or inns out in the countryside, many of which are included in the tours. Each route is around 20 miles in length which allows time for visiting attractions, strolling round villages and sampling the unrivalled range of gastronomic delights the region has to offer.

Bear in mind that traffic on main roads such as the A40 and A429 can be heavy in summer, especially at weekends, although the routes in this book are mainly along quiet back roads and lanes. However, some country lanes are quite narrow and passing oncoming vehicles is often a matter of negotiation. This is all part of the Cotswold experience and should be enjoyed and appreciated.

Take care and happy motoring!

Jim Watson

Rugby 2019

Hampnett

Chipping Campden to Moreton-in-Marsh · 20 miles

Chipping Campden – Hidcote Boyce – Ilmington – Charingworth – Ebrington – Paxford – Blockley – Bourton-on-the-Hill – Moreton-in-Marsh.

ATTRACTIONS

1 Kiftsgate Court Gardens
2 Hidcote
3 Mill Dene Garden
4 Batsford Arboretum
5 Sezincote

Most of the attractions have small shops and cafés or tearooms

VILLAGE INNS

6 Red Lion, Ilmington
7 Howard Arms, Ilmington
8 Ebrington Arms, Ebrington
9 Churchill Arms, Paxford
10 Great Western Arms, Blockley
11 Crown Inn, Blockley
12 Horse & Groom, Bourton-on-the-Hill

VILLAGE SHOPS & CAFÉS

13 Ilmington
14 Blockley

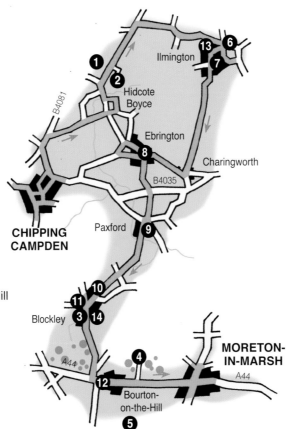

This tour begins at Chipping Campden, one of the great set piece Cotswolds towns. We head north to two world-famous gardens and on to Ilmington, most northerly of the Cotswold villages. Returning south we climb Windmill Hill for expansive views before descending through open farmland to Ebrington, with its multi award-winning inn and thatched cottages. We continue south to Paxford, which despite being only a small hamlet boasts a high-end menu at the local pub, The Churchill. Blockley is a large village, once the centre of a prosperous 19th-century silk industry and an excellent place to park and explore. Quiet country roads and lanes now give way to the busy A44, going through delightful Bourton-on-the-Hill and passing two more major horticultural attractions, Sezincote and Batsford Arboretum, before ending the tour at the market town of Moreton-in-Marsh.

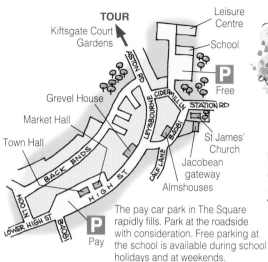

Market Hall on High Street

The pay car park in The Square rapidly fills. Park at the roadside with consideration. Free parking at the school is available during school holidays and at weekends.

Chipping Campden

Situated high on the escarpment, and loveliest of all the Cotswold towns, Chipping Campden is famed for its architecture, history, feel-good character and hospitality. The town dates back to the 12th century when it was an important trading centre. During the late Middle Ages, Cotswold wool was a famous commodity throughout Western Europe.

Make time for a stroll up and down the elegant High Street where, apart from the parked cars, everything is worth a look. Substantial buildings line the mile-long

street, each with its own distinct design but also part of the wondrous whole. Many date from the 14th century and their honey-coloured stone still retains the glow of prosperity and well-being.

Campden's bijou Town Hall occupies an island site on the edge of the small square. It's of uncertain age but parts date back to the 14th century. The building incorporates two buttresses, the only remaining parts of St Katherine's Chapel, built in 1180. A plaque on one corner marks the beginning (or end) of the Cotswold Way, a long-distance footpath that follows the escarpment all the way to Bath, one hundred miles south.

Town Hall

7

Grevel House

North-west side of High Street

The striking Market Hall in High Street, was a gift to the town by Sir Baptist Hicks in 1627 as a shelter for traders selling butter, cheese and poultry. Its simple design – five open arches long by two wide – and uneven floor of well-worn stones provides us an authentic glimpse of what life must have been like in a 17th-century Cotswold village.

Hicks, a wealthy textile merchant, was Member of Parliament for Tavistock and Tewkesbury, and in 1626 was made Viscount Campden.

Market Hall

An earlier resident, William Grevel, built Grevel House with its gargoyles, sundial and slender bay widows around 1390. His family had lived in Campden for many years and made their fortune in the wool trade.

Across the road from Grevel House stands The Woolstaplers' Hall, built a few years earlier by another wealthy wool-trader, Robert Calf, as a place for merchants to gather and buy staples of Cotswold wool.

High Street boasts fine examples of Tudor, Jacobean and Georgian façades, but artfully hidden behind them are state-of-the-art hotels, boutiques and yes, even ordinary shops!

South-east side of High Street

St James' Church tower

Campden House gateway

Sir Baptist Hicks, a founder of the East India Company and one of the richest men in the country, was the town's greatest benefactor. He built Campden House in 1613, a flamboyant italian-style mansion, which was destroyed by the Royalist Hicks family during the Civil War (1641-51) to prevent it falling into the hands of Oliver Cromwell's Parliamentarians. The Jacobean lodges and gateway fronting open fields are all that remain today. Hicks further ensured his legacy by donating the pulpit and lectern in St James' Church, where he is grandly interred in the family chapel.

There was a Norman church on this site before 1180 but it took another 300 years before St James' began to look anything like the archetypical Cotswold wool church it does today. The airy nave was reconstructed about 1490 and the 120ft (36m) high west tower added around 1500.

Food & Drink

Chipping Campden is particularly well-blessed with eating and drinking establishments. This is only a tiny guide on what the town has to offer:

The **Kings Hotel** overlooks the square and offers brunch, lunch, cream tea or full evening meal.

The popular **Eight Bells Inn** in Church Street provides a genuine old English experience with open fires and candlelit tables plus a choice of local ales and ciders on tap and the finest seasonal produce.

Housed in a five-hundred-year-old building, **Huxleys** boasts a wonderful terrace overlooking the town square. It's an intimate café and wine bar with old oak beams, a roaring log fire in winter and comfy leather sofas.

Buttys at the lower end of High Street prepare fresh sandwiches, breakfast baguettes and salad boxes made while you wait.

For something completely different try **Michael's Mediterranean**, a Greek restaurant on High Street with a string of good reviews.

The Tour

Leave Chipping Campden at the northeast end of the town on the B4035. When the road forks take the right hand B4081 signed Hidcote, then the next right into narrow Furze Lane signed Hidcote Boyce. Cross farmland for about 1½ miles. At the crossroads go straight across, ignoring the sign to Hidcote Bartram, then take the next left through the pleasant hamlet of Hidcote Boyce. At the T-junction at the end of the single street turn right, signed Hidcote Gardens and Kiftsgate Court.

Situated on the edge of the Cotswold Scarp, Kiftsgate Court Gardens were laid out after the First World War by Mrs Heather Muir. Her daughter and granddaughter have continued the development and the family still live in the house. Kiftsgate House is largely Victorian, with a remarkable 18th-century portico, transported piece by piece from Mickleton Manor on a specially constructed light railway.

Kiftsgate Court

Hidcote

❶ Kiftsgate Court Gardens

Magnificent situation with stunning views. Rare shrubs, plants and an exceptional collection of roses, including the largest rose bush in England. Water garden and tearoom. Gift and plant shop.

Open: check website
Admission charge
Tel: 01386 438777
www.kiftsgate.co.uk

❷ Hidcote

World-famous garden with a seasonal colourful tapestry of narrow paths, secret spots and intricately designed 'rooms'. Café, shop and plant centre.

Open: check website
Admission charge
Tel: 01386 438333
www.nationaltrust.org.uk/hidcote

Hidcote is an Arts & Crafts masterpiece, often described as 'the greatest garden of the 20th century'. It was created from eleven acres of largely open Cotswold hill country around a 17th-century manor house by the revered horticulturist, Major Lawrence Johnston, who dedicated 40 years of his life to its creation.

The estate was the first property acquired by the National Trust (in 1947), said to be purely for its garden. The views of distant Bredon Hill and the Malverns across the valleys of the Severn and Avon also draw the crowds. A keen gardener could happily spend all day here.

From Kiftsgate Court continue on the straight and narrow road ahead for about a mile to a T-junction. Bear right here into Admington Lane, signed Ilmington. Stay on this road for around two miles into the village.

Looking to Frog Lane

Ilmington

Situated in the far north of the Cotswolds – actually in Warwickshire – Ilmington is a widespread, handsome and welcoming village at the foot of Ilmington Downs. Its wealth of old houses and cottages – an attractive mixture of stone and brick, thatch and slate – have mellowed over the years to picturesque perfection. The village is criss-crossed by a tangle of minor roads, lanes and footpaths. An hour or so exploring their nooks and crannies will never be time wasted.

St Mary's Church

St Mary the Virgin Church on Back Street has existed in some form since the early 11th century and its Norman belltower is considered to be one of the finest in Warwickshire. Its peal of eight bells have been heard on Radio 4.

The church's oak pews were carved by the Yorkshire furniture-maker Robert Thompson and have 11 of his trademark carved mice hidden amongst them. The embroided Apple Map (a copy of medieval maps) is another church treasure, which celebrates the 38 varieties of apples grown in the village. St Mary's is open daily from 9am.

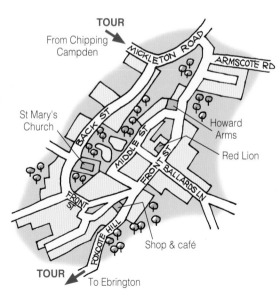

TOUR
From Chipping Campden
MICKLETON ROAD
ARMSCOTE RD
St Mary's Church
BACK ST
MIDDLE ST
FRONT ST
BALLARDS LN
Howard Arms
Red Lion
FRONT ST
FOXCOTE HILL
Shop & café
TOUR
To Ebrington

The Red Lion serves Hook Norton beer from the local brewery near Chipping Norton, quality craft ales, and a huge range of artisan gins from all over the world.

As a non-alcoholic antidote try their Grizzly Bear coffee, made from ethically produced Arabica beans. There's also weekly live music nights, with the landlord often joining in on guitar.

The Red Lion

The Howard Arms

❻ Red Lion

Traditional village pub with the emphasis on drinking and banter with friends. Simple bar snacks available that are 'quick to serve but wholesome and tasty'. Dog friendly.

Open for food: Fri-Sun noon-2.30pm
Tue-Sat 6-8.30pm
Tel: 01608 682089
www.theredlionilmington.co.uk

❼ Howard Arms

Popular 400-year-old Cotswold stone inn and restaurant with eight luxury bed & breakfast rooms overlooking the peaceful village green. Acclaimed for the quality of its menus, Sunday roasts and hearty breakfasts.

Open: Mon-Sat 11am-11pm
Sun noon-10.30pm
Tel: 01608 682226
www.howardarms.com

The Howard Arms is named after the Lordship of Ilmington Manor which resides with Lord Howard of Corby, a member of the Flowers family who still reside in the Manor. Edward Fordham Flowers founded Flowers Brewery in Stratford-upon-Avon in 1831 and his son, Charles, was founder of the original Shakespeare Theatre in 1875.

The main building of the Howard Arms dates from the late 16th century and has a bar with a low ceiling and a shiny flagstone floor. The Stratford Gold Ale is particularly recommended. The pub also has an attractive back garden with picnic tables scattered across the lawn. It featured in *The Times* 'Britain's 30 best summer pubs' in 2018.

Situated in the former Catholic Church on the Upper Green, Ilmington shop and café is a community owned cooperative owned by around half of the over 700 village population, who bought shares with a minimum investment of £10. All members have an equal say in how the business is run, irrespective of their level of investment. A team of volunteers welcome visitors, walkers and cyclists seven days a week, with the café closed on Mondays.

Apart from its more obvious picturesque attributes the village was for many years also acclaimed as the home of Morris Dancing, an ancient rural pursuit which involves bells, handkerchiefs, flowered hats and the banging of sticks, accompanied by a melodeon and performed outdoors, predictably close to a pub.

In one respect (and only one!) captivating Ilmington is like Morris Dancing – once seen, never forgotten.

Ilmington shop and café

Leave Ilmington, climbing Foxcote Hill past the shop to some fabulous views across open countryside. Beyond Southfield Farm take the left turn at an unsigned tee junction. Continue with more expansive views to the hamlet of Charingworth.

Turn right at the tee junction and at the fork take the right hand (upper) road, signed further along as the road to Ebrington. Turn left on the outskirts of the village, signed Ebrington ¼ and Chipping Campden 2¾.

The view east from Windmill Hill

Charingworth

Ebrington thatch

❽ Ebrington Arms

This delightful 17th-century inn has won a clutch of CAMRA Pub of the Year awards, featured in the *Good Food Guide* and was rated 'The UK's number one village pub' by *The Times* in 2017. It also has its own craft beer range, serves fine food and boasts five luxurious B&B rooms. Traditional in style with flagstones, low beams and roaring fires.

Open: Daily 9am until close
Tel: 01386 593223
www.theebringtonarms.co.uk

Ebrington

An attractive hillside village, known to many locals as 'Yubberton', Ebrington dates back to the 1400s, while the local church, St Eadburgh's, has Saxon foundations and is noted in the *Domesday Book*. The highly-rated primary school dates to Victorian times.

Ebrington Manor has been home to the Fortesque family since the 15th century. There are many monuments to the family in the church, including one to Sir John Fortescue in his robes as Lord Chief Justice.

Head to the centre of the village where there's a small tree-shaded green and the multi award-winning Ebrington Arms. Turn right here and climb the hill past a series of picturesque thatched cottages to the village hall, where you can park and take in the wonderful views across the rolling Cotswold hills.

Ebrington Arms

Turn left down May Lane passing the pub and go over the B4035 into an unclassified road signed Paxford 1¼. Turn right at the next T-junction to Paxford. Swing left through the small settlement, following a sign 'Blockley 2'. Where the road forks, take the narrow one left, signed Aston Magna. This takes you along the tightly packed and bendy village street to the picturesque Churchill Arms and the pretty little Paxford Mission Church across the road. Turn left past the church and continue along the B4479.

Paxford

 Churchill Arms, Paxford

Award-winning owner and head chef, Nick Deverell-Smith offers quality modern cuisine in this 17th-century village pub. There's also elegant en-suite bedrooms and predictably a beer named after the Great Man himself.

Open: Tue to Sat 12.30-3pm & 6-9pm. Sun noon-4pm
Closed Mondays
Tel: 01386 593159
www.churchillarms.com

The Churchill Arms and Paxford Mission Church

Go over a railway crossing and pass Northcot brick works. A further 1¼ miles brings you to Blockley, a village worthy of a stop and walk around. Go past the Great Western Arms and turn right into St George's terrace, then turn left signed 'Blockley village only'. You may be able to park at the roadside in Bell Lane by the park. The village has no official car park.

Blockley

Once the centre of a prosperous 19th-century silk industry, this large, handsome village of Cotswold stone is tiered on the steep slopes of the high wolds above a rushing brook. The church of St Peter & St Paul has a Norman chancel, three 15th-century windows and a Jacobean pulpit. The Gothic tower was added around 1725 by the local quarry-owner, Thomas Woodward. The medieval bishops of Worcester, wisely made Blockley their summer residence.

Church of St Peter & St Paul

A substantial terrace of mainly 18th and early 19th-century houses flows down the hill from the church to the Crown Hotel. There was once 20 shops in this now quiet street and the village had eight pubs.

Blockley boasts a community run shop and café, and the village is an interesting and attractive place to walk around – but you do have to like hills!

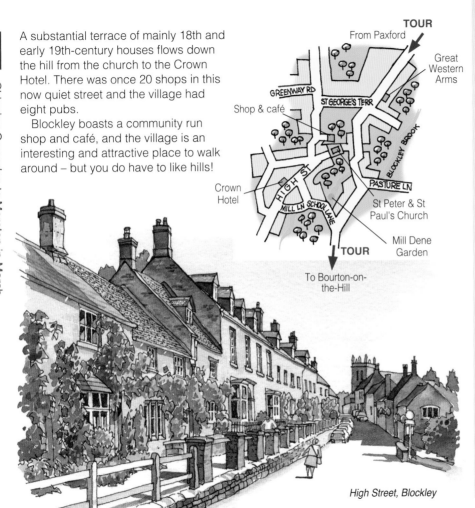

High Street, Blockley

❿ Great Western Arms

Village local with hearty pub grub and local ales from Hook Norton Brewery.

Open: Check website
Tel: 01386 700362
www.thegreatwesternarms.co.uk

⓫ Crown Hotel

Set in an ancient building with old world comfort and service, the Crown boasts 24 en-suite bedrooms and the 'Rafters' restaurant.

Open: Phone for details
Tel: 01386 700245
www.crownhotelblockley.co.uk

❸ Mill Dene Garden

Another garden, but this one is on a more intimate and personal scale. It's described as 'witty, surprising and beautiful, as well as being horticulturally excellent'. Here you can chill out with a cream tea by the tranquil mill pond with trout, ducks and the resident kingfisher for company. Small car park.

Open: check website
Admission charge
Tel: 01386 700457
www.milldenegarden.co.uk

Return to the B4479 crossroads near the Great Western Arms and turn right, going down the hill signed Bourton-on-the-Hill. At a T- junction turn left onto the busy A44, signed Oxford. Pass the Horse & Groom and go down the hill through the village.

The Horse and Groom

Bourton-on-the-Hill

⓬ Horse and Groom

Long-established in a handsome Georgian building of Cotswold stone, this award-winning and hugely popular free house has a fine reputation for classic British cuisine and the laid back charm of a traditional Cotswold country pub. There's five sumptuous bedrooms, log fires in the winter and a welcome for dogs in the main bar areas.

Open: Check website
Tel: 01386 700413
www.horseandgroom.info

Once owned by the Abbots of Westminster, who kept large flocks of sheep on nearby Bourton Downs, Bourton-on-the-Hill developed in the 17th century. It's located on a steep hill, once part of the turnpiked London, Oxford and Worcester 'Great Road', now the busy and noisy A44.

Pretty terraces of classic Cotswold cottages line the roadside, clustered around the warm stone of St Lawrence's Church. Bourton House stands at the bottom of the hill with a fine barn dated 1570 in the gardens, which are occasionally open to the public.

Cottages on the A44

St Lawrence's Church

St Lawrence's Church dates back to 1157, though it's been altered and added to over the centuries. Massive columns inside the building reveal its Norman origins.

A clock in the tower was installed in 1904 to replace one that had been there since 1686 and a peal of six bells dates from 1677 to 1873.

Parking is possible with consideration in the streets off Main Street but, apart from the splendid Horse & Groom, the village has no other facilities.

Continue along the A44 and you soon reach the long driveway to Batsford Arboretum leading off to the left. The lodge entrance to Sezincote House is opposite. Another mile or so along the A44 brings you to the end of this tour at Moreton-in-Marsh.

Sezincote House

❹ Batsford Arboretum

The country's largest private collection of trees and shrubs, spread attractively across 56 acres of hilly countryside. Originally set out in the Chinese and Japanese wild style by Algernon Freeman-Mitford, grandfather of the Mitford sisters who later lived at the house during World War One. Café and gift shop.

Open daily Mon-Sat: 9am-5pm
Sun 10am-5pm
Admission charge to arboretum
Tel: 01386 701441
www.batsarb.co.uk.co.uk

❺ Sezincote House & Garden

Part of a 4,500 acre, family-run estate, Sezincote House is an amazing 200-year-old Mogul Indian palace, set in a romantic landscape of temples, grottoes, waterfalls and canals reminiscent of the Taj Mahal and said to be the inspiration for Brighton Pavilion.

Restricted opening
Check website for times
Admission charge (credit and debit cards are not accepted)
Tel: 01386 700444
www.sezincote.co.uk

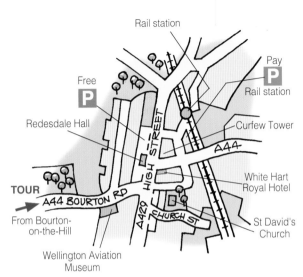

Rail station

Pay
P
Rail station

Free
P

Redesdale Hall

Curfew Tower

A44

TOUR
A44 BOURTON RD

A429

HIGH STREET

CHURCH ST

White Hart
Royal Hotel

St David's
Church

From Bourton-
on-the-Hill

Wellington Aviation
Museum

Moreton-in-Marsh

Situated on the cross roads of the Roman Fosse Way, now the A429, and the A44, the main road between Worcester and Oxford, the unusually wide High Street of the town of Moreton-in-Marsh has been busy with traffic between the Midlands and the south-west for centuries. Modern traffic is even heavier and the town's stone-built shops, houses and old coaching inns face each other across a frequently crowded highway.

Moreton developed as a market town in the 1220s, and 18th-century turnpike road building brought increased prosperity. Local Inns provided changes of horses for the coaching trade with lodgings for drivers and passengers, usually the nobility. Many of the fine buildings in the High Street date from this period. Business boomed from 1853 when the Oxford, Worcester and Wolverhampton Railway opened with a station in the town, which now provides a direct link to London. A market is still held in the High Street on Tuesdays.

Parking in the town can be difficult but you can usually park (currently free) in the High Street on non-market days. Avoid Bank Holidays.

Houses in High Street

19

Once surrounded by low-level, swampy land, Moreton was often flooded, which may explain the present name (never Moreton-in-THE-Marsh!). Despite major work over the years to protect it, heavy rain brought flooding to parts of the town as recently as 2007.

The White Hart Royal Hotel occupies a corner site with its front door on High Street and a side entrance on Oxford Street. This is the oldest part of town, established in the early 1200s by the abbots of Worcester, who owned the land. Formally The White Hart, the hotel dates to the 1400s with its original wattle-and daub construction still visible inside. Charles I is known to have sheltered here on two occasions during the Civil war. The Mann institute across the road in Oxford Street was built by Miss Edith Mann, in memory of her father, Dr John Mann (son of the first Congregational minister), as a working men's club in 1802.

A striking Palladian townhouse, the Steps, at the southern end of High Street, was built in the mid-18th century, while the Curfew Tower on the corner of Oxford Street dates back to the Norman Conquest. The bell, dated 1633, was rung nightly until the 1860s to order people back to their homes to 'cover fire' for the night. It was also at one time the town's 'lock-up' (jail).

Curfew Tower

High Street

Mann Institute

Curfew Tower

White Hart Royal Hotel

Food & Drink

Mainly on High Street. **The Black Bear**, a traditional pub, serves above average food and Donnington Ales. For light meals or traditional cream teas try **Marshmallow** or the **Cotswold Tea Company**. If Artisan Gelato floats your boat, head for the **Yellow Brick Café** just off High Street, while the **Mulberry**, situated at the posh Manor House Hotel, offers highly acclaimed modern British cuisine – with prices to match.

A Victorian Tudor building, Redesdale Hall, dominates the High Street like a beached ocean liner. Built around 1887, it was designed by the architect Ernest George and presented to the town by Lord Dulverton of Batsford in memory of his kinsman, the Earl of Redesdale. Owned by the Parish Council since 1974, it can be hired for events. George VI reviewed the Airborne Division outside the hall before the Normandy landings in 1944.

St David's Church, lying east of the High Street, is almost entirely Victorian and generally considered to be of little interest to visitors. However, the quirky Wellington Aviation Museum, situated just out of town on the A44, displays memorabilia from Moreton's wartime RAF base (including bits of planes) and is worth a visit. But it does have quirky opening times too!

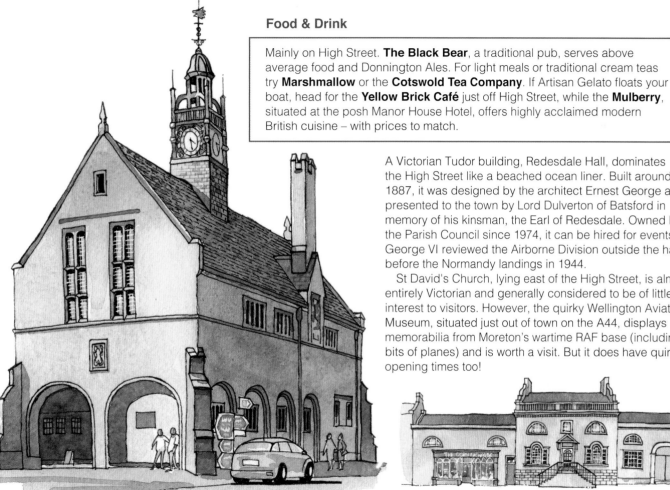

Redesdale Hall

The Steps

Winchcombe to Broadway · 23 miles

Winchcombe – Stanton – Stanway – Snowshill – Broadway Tower – Broadway

ATTRACTIONS

1. Sudley Castle
2. Hailes Abbey
3. Hayles Fruit Farm
4. Gloucestershire Warwickshire Railway
5. Stanway House
6. Snowshill Manor
7. Cotswold Lavender
8. Broadway Tower

Most of the attractions have small shops and cafés.

VILLAGE INNS

9. Pheasant Inn, Toddington
10. Mount Inn, Stanton
11. Snowshill Arms, Snowshill

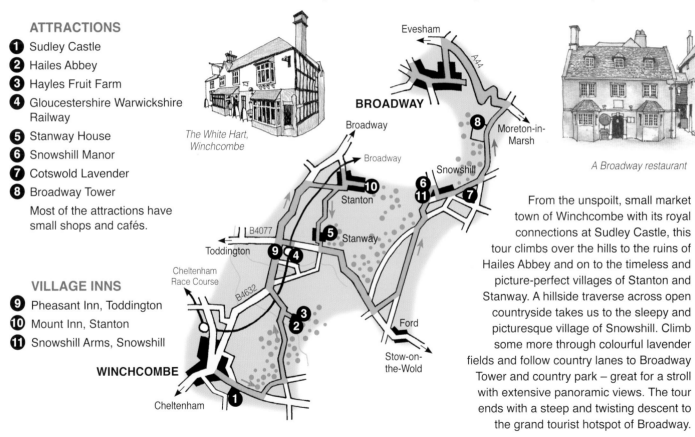

The White Hart, Winchcombe

A Broadway restaurant

From the unspoilt, small market town of Winchcombe with its royal connections at Sudley Castle, this tour climbs over the hills to the ruins of Hailes Abbey and on to the timeless and picture-perfect villages of Stanton and Stanway. A hillside traverse across open countryside takes us to the sleepy and picturesque village of Snowshill. Climb some more through colourful lavender fields and follow country lanes to Broadway Tower and country park – great for a stroll with extensive panoramic views. The tour ends with a steep and twisting descent to the grand tourist hotspot of Broadway.

Winchcombe

Sheltered on three sides by high Cotswolds hills, the small market town of Winchcombe is situated along the western bank of the River Isbourne. With old cottages, small independent shops, a rich history and some good pubs and tea-rooms, there's plenty for the visitor to enjoy.

During Saxon times Winchcombe was the wool capital of Mercia, a separate shire. Later it became the site of one of the largest Benedictine monasteries in England and a place of pilgrimage for the rich and powerful. During Henry VIII's Dissolution of the Monastries (1536-41) the abbey was totally destroyed and not a trace of it remains above ground.

With the resultant loss of visiting pilgrims and employment, Winchcombe was plunged into poverty. The townsfolk turned to crafts to make a living, even growing tobacco for a while.

The Town Hall in Hailes Street was brick-built in Tudor style in 1853 and enlarged in 1871. It now houses the folk and Police museum. There's also several Tudor houses in the street with exposed timber-framing and overhung first floors. North Street has some interesting buildings, including the 17th-century White Lion and an old brewery house. Gloucester Street, at the west end of the town beyond the church, is also lined with ancient buildings.

Hailes Street and Winchcombe Folk & Police Museum

The cheery Sudeley Almshouses, built in 1865 (off Abbey Terrace) to a design by Sir Gilbert Scott, are a delight with their patterns of different coloured stone.

There's also a wonderful string of cottages on Vineyard Street going down to the river, where a ducking stool for 'gossipers' was kept at the waterside during the 18th century.

Abbey Terrace

The galleried yard of the former George Inn

The former George Inn, across the road from the Folk & Police Museum, was built by the abbey as an inn for pilgrims. The doorway has carved in its spandrels the initials of Abbot Richard Kidderminster, who resigned due to ill health in 1525. An open gallery has been preserved in the narrow courtyard behind. The inn was closed in 1988 and converted into apartments. The inn's sign is on display in the Winchcombe museum.

Food & Drink

If you fancy a cuppa try **Juri's Tearoom** in High Street or select from a variety of sausage dishes at **Wine and Sausages** in the **White Hart**. For something even more substantial head for **The Lion Inn**, a former 15th-century coaching inn in North Street.

Lion Inn

In an early example of a private and public joint building project, the chancel of the large Perpendicular Church of St Peter was built by the abbey around the 1460s, while the parish was responsible for building the nave. Despite the involvement of the abbey, the church miraculously survived the Dissolution.

An altar cloth, said to have been stitched by Catherine of Aragon (first wife of Henry VIII) when she visited Sudeley Castle, is displayed in the church. There are 40 gargoyles on the building's exterior, believed to represent local characters from the 1460s.

Jacobean House, set in a small square near the church, is a superb example of a typical 17th-century merchant's house.

Beautifully situated amid a magnificent estate across the river from Winchcombe and looking across the valley to the wooded slopes of Cleeve Hill, Sudeley Castle is renowned for its long and fascinating history and beautiful gardens.

Anne Boleyn, the second of Henry VIII's wives, visited Sudeley and Katherine Parr, his sixth and last wife came to live here after his death in 1547. She quickly remarried but died in childbirth in 1549 and is buried in St Mary's Church. Sudley is the only castle in private ownership to have a queen buried in its grounds.

During the English Civil War, the castle acted as a Royalist garrison and was badly damaged, falling into virtual ruin. More than a century later, in 1837, the Dent family bought the estate and began a remarkable restoration led by the formidable Emma Dent, who also funded new roads and provided Winchcombe with its first piped water supply to celebrate Queen Victoria's Golden Jubilee. Her descendants still live in the castle.

❶ Sudeley Castle

Royal connections stretching back over 1,000 years. Stunning scenery, exhibitions, a magnificent play area, two cafés and the largest rare breed pheasantry in Europe . Free access to visitor centre with parking. Entrance down Vineyard Street off Winchcombe High Street.

Open daily April - October 10am-5pm.
Admission charge
Tel: 01242 604244
www.sudleycastle.co.uk

Jacobean House and St Peter's Church

Sudley Castle gatehouse on Castle Road

🚗 The Tour

Begin on Hailes Street and turn into narrow Castle Street by the White Hart Inn, heading east. Pass the gatehouse to Sudely Castle and begin to climb Sudely Hill. Just beyond a small wood turn left onto an unclassified road signed Ford 3¼. Continue climbing across the hillside with terrific views back across Winchcome. At 970ft, one of the highest points in the area, turn left signed Little Farmcote. Begin to descend, and where the road splits take the left, unfenced side (Salter's Lane). After about a mile swing right to a well-signed junction on your right for the no entry lane to Hailes Abbey.

Hailes Abbey

Hailes Abbey was once one of England's great Cistercian monastries founded in 1246 by Richard, Earl of Cornwall, King Henry III's brother. Pilgrims travelled from far and wide to worship before the *Holy Blood of Hailes*, allegedly the blood of Christ. The relic was denounced as a fake in 1538 and a year later the abbey itself was demolished as part of Henry VIII's Dissolution. Only weather-beaten cloister arches and grassy foundations survive. However, the recently refurbished onsite museum vividly brings to life 300 years of piety, culture and tradition.

Hailes Church, across the road, is actually a century older than the abbey and though originally a parish church, served as its chapel after the isolation-loving Cistercians banished the villagers to nearby Didbrook. The atmospheric church contains a unique collection of unrestored medieval wall paintings.

Hayles Fruit Farm nearby is famed for its apples and pears and is an excellent place to stop, browse in the shop and maybe enjoy tea in the garden, or even sample the local speciality, Badger's Bottom Cider.

❷ Hailes Abbey

Ruins of 13th-century Cistercian abbey. Museum and audio tour.

Open daily from 10am, Easter to end of October
Admission charge
Tel: 01242 602398
www.english-heritage.org.uk/hailes

❸ Hayles Fruit Farm

Onsite apple juice and cider production, shop and tearoom. Also coarse fishing, a family-friendly nature trail and campsite for tents and caravans.

Tearoom open daily 9am - 5pm
Tel: 01242 602123
www.haylesfruitfarm.co.uk

According to farm staff the original spelling of the location was 'Hayles' and English Heritage changed it to 'Hailes' when they took over the abbey in 1936.

Hailes Church

Return to Salter's Lane and turn right across flat farmland. Go over the railway and at the T-junction turn right onto the B4632, signed Stratford. Another mile further brings you to the Torrington roundabout, with the Pheasant Inn on your right. For the short detour to visit the Gloucestershire Warwickshire Railway station, turn right onto the B4077.

Pheasant Inn

Gloucester Warwickshire railway

❾ Pheasant Inn, Toddington

Family friendly traditional pub with locally sourced home cooked food, including breakfasts. Donnington Ales. Situated next to the railway station.

Tel: 01242 621271
www.thepheasantinntoddington.co.uk

❹ Gloucestershire Warwickshire Railway

The 'Heritage Line in the Cotswolds' offering 25 mile round trips on a scenic route through prime Cotswold countryside. Free car parking, Flag and Whistle café, small shop, heritage trail and picnic area. Trains run most of the year, most frequently during the summer.

Tel: 01242 621405
www.gwsr.com

Gloucester Warwickshire railway is a volunteer-run heritage railway that runs along the former Honeybourne Line, part of the old Great Western Railway. The original line, opened in 1906, was closed in 1976.

New track laying by the preservation group began in 1981 and continues to this day, with an extension to Broadway opened in 2018. The line is now 14 miles long with stations at Cheltenham Racecourse, Gotherington, Winchcombe, Hailes Abbey and Toddington. The route includes a 15 arch viaduct at Stanway, and Greet Tunnel, at 693 yards (634m) long, the second longest on any heritage line.

The railway operates a wide variety of steam and heritage diesel locomotives. These have included the world-famous locomotive *The Flying Scotsman* and the celebrated *City of Truro,* which in 1904, was the first engine to reach 100 mph.

Return to the Toddington roundabout and take the B4632 on your right signed Broadway 5. After around 1½ miles, turn right into an unclassified road, signed Stanton.

Stanton

An outstandingly beautiful village snuggled below wooded Shenberrow Hill, Stanton is claimed to be one of the oldest settlements in the Cotswolds. Entirely built of warm Cotswold stone, It's certainly one of the most attractive, thanks largely to Sir Philip Stott, an architect who acquired the estate in 1906.

Until his death in 1937, he spent much of his time and fortune on the restoration of Stanton's houses and cottages many of which were in a delapidated state after years of neglect.

Hard to believe in today's genteel surroundings, this was once an impoverished workhorse for the 17th-century hose-making industry; many villagers died in an epidemic fever that swept the Cotswolds in 1728.

A magnificent converted barn stands at the centre of the village, still known as Sheppey Corner from the time when sheep from the hills were gathered here for shearing.

Apart from the one for patron's only at the Mount Inn, Stanton has no public car park. Parking is only possible with consideration at the roadside.

Sheppey Corner

St Michael's church is tucked away up an alley behind the medieval village cross. Of Norman origins, as seen in the spire and north arcade, there are also traces of early 14th-century wall paintings. The interior of the building was severely damaged during the Civil War when, like other Cotswold churches, it was used to house prisoners. Beautiful wood carvings were used as firewood and many windows smashed.

Walk beyond the old wayside cross, climbing the long main street through an avenue of local stone houses, with mullioned windows and Jacobean gables lined up in homogeneous perfection. Keep climbing to the Mount Inn, from where there's a fantastic view back across the village rooftops.

The view across the rooftops

⑩ Mount Inn

Seventeenth-century inn serving Donnington Ales with traditional pub food and traditional opening times: Tue – Sat: noon–3pm & 6–11pm. Sunday noon-4pm only. The view is worth the steep climb – even when the pub's closed.

Tel: 011386 584316
www.themountinn.co.uk

Mount Inn

Head back through the village and take the unclassified road going left that you passed earlier, signed Stanway. This takes you through open farmland into the Stanway estate.

Main Street

Stanway

A huge Jacobean manor house, Stanway House, dominates this small settlement. It was built around 1600 by Sir Paul Tracy and includes a remarkable 60-pane full height bay window. Much of the furniture is original, including a 22ft-long shuffleboard table built in 1620. The rooms have an amiable lived-in character, which is hardly surprising as the same family have lived in the house since it was built.

A magnificent tithe barn in the grounds dates to around 1370 and a restored water garden has the highest gravity-fed fountain in the world which can reach a height of 300 feet when all the valves are open. There's also a restored 13th-century watermill.

The gateway to the house is oddly built at the side of the house rather than the front entrance. Its flamboyant design in buttery Cotswold stone was for years attributed to Inigo Jones, but is now thought to be the work of a local mason, Timothy Strong.

❺ Stanway House

Splendid manor house with unusual and eccentric attractions, plus a tearoom. Still lived in by Lord and Lady Neidpath (the Earl and Countess of Wemyss) so opening times are restricted to 2–5pm on Tuesdays and Thursdays during June, July and August. Worth checking out.

Admission charge
Tel: 01386 584469
www.stanwayfountain.co.uk

Stanway House gateway

Stanway House

Cricket pavilion

Leaving Stanway at the junction with the B4077 you pass an unusual war memorial, the work of three distinguished Victorians. The bronze of *St George and the Dragon* is by silversmith and painter, Alexander Fisher, the stone column and plinth by architect and civil engineer, Sir Philip Stott, and the lettering was carved by sculptor and typeface designer Eric Gill. Both Fisher and Gill were involved with the Arts and Crafts movement.

War memorial

As you enter Stanway look out for a thatched cricket pavilion, clad with larch poles and raised on saddle stones, a surprising sight in these parkland surroundings. It was presented to Stanway by J.M. Barrie, the author of *Peter Pan*, who was a keen cricketer and a frequent visitor to Stanway House during the early 1900s. A local 'fairy' story has it that moonlight flickering on his bedroom wall inspired Barrie's creation of Tinkerbell.

Equally hypothetical is the story that the cricket field's undulating surface was to deter German gliders from landing during WWII.

St Peter's Church stands in magnificent surroundings next to the gatehouse and dates to the 12th century. Said to be have been 'over-restored' by the Victorians, the interior has a Jacobean pulpit and a beautiful little bronze by Alexander Fisher, one of the sculptors of the nearby *St George and the Dragon* memorial.

Parking is possible outside the church but, apart from Stanway House, the village has no facilities.

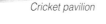
From Stanway turn left onto the B4077 signed Stow. Stay on this road for around 2½ miles, then, at a crossroads, turn left signed Cutsdean ½ and Snowshill 3. At the next crossroads turn left, signed Snowshill 2¼. Continue through open countryside passing a couple of farms at Taddington until you reach an unfenced road, signed Snowshill & Broadway, going left. This takes you down a wooded hill into the village of Snowshill.

Snowshill

Overlooking the Avon valley and the Midland Plain, Snowshill is a wonderfully disordered village, built on a hillside so that hardly a building is on the same level as its neighbour. The history of the small settlement stretches back over 1,000 years when the King of Mercia gave the manor to Winchcombe Abbey. At the Dissolution Henry VIII transferred ownership to his sixth wife, Katherine Parr.

The Church of St Barnabas stands surrounded by a walled churchyard at the centre of the village, in perfect harmony with the terraces of ancient cottages. Surprisingly it's largely a solid Victorian rebuild of 1864 with enormously thick walls. A beautiful 15th-century octagonal font and a 17th-century carved pulpit were retained from the original building.

The Snowshill Arms is opposite. A traditional village inn dating back to the 13th century, it has a large car park and 'welcomes all-comers'.

With its array of traditional Cotswold architecture and open aspect, Snowshill is a delight to explore. The peaceful valleys and windswept hills of the surrounding countryside are equally attractive for walkers or riding enthusiasts

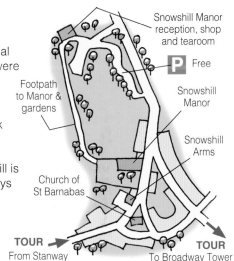

Snowshill Manor reception, shop and tearoom

P Free

Snowshill Manor

Footpath to Manor & gardens

Snowshill Arms

Church of St Barnabas

TOUR From Stanway

TOUR To Broadway Tower

Looking east across the village

Snowshill Manor

Snowshill Manor, built in traditional Cotswold style with a William & Mary front during the 1500s, was bought by Charles Paget Wade soon after World War I. He took a delight in filling it with his unlikely treasures. 'Let nothing perish' was his motto and his collection celebrates craftsmanship and design.

Every room in the house is packed with bygone curios; toys, tools, musical instruments, even bicycles. Wade refused modern amenities and lived in the humble Priest's House nearby, sleeping in a Tudor cupboard-bed.

After donating the Manor to the National Trust in 1951, Wade went to live in the West Indies with his wife. He died on a visit to England in 1956 and is buried in the village graveyard with other members of his family.

Helped by his fellow architect, Baillie Scott, Wade designed the extensive garden as a series of outdoor rooms, including Wolf's Cove, a model village.

A large car park, almost hidden by trees, serves both the village and the Manor. You need to go though reception to access the House then walk 500 yards up a steep hill into the garden. A free buggy ride is available on request on open days.

❻ Snowshill Manor

Unique 22,000-item collection of one man's treasures packed into a Cotswold manor house with a large terraced garden. Shop and tearoom. Large car park.

Open April to October. Check website.
Admission charge
Tel: 01386 852410
www.nationaltrust.org/snowshillmanor

⓫ Snowshill Arms

Popular, family-friendly (including dogs), inn dating back to the 13th century. Large play area and log fires in the winter. Pub grub and Donnington Ales. Cosy.

Open daily 11am-3pm & 6-11pm
Tel: 01386 852653
www.donnington-brewery.com

❼ Cotswold Lavender

Set on a sunny hillside above Snowshill, a colourful 53 acres of fragrance. Gift shop and lavender scones in the tearoom.

Open daily mid-June to mid-August, 10am-5pm
Tel: 01386 854821
www.cotswoldlavender.co.uk

Leave Snowshill at the northern end of the village, signed Cotswold Lavender. Climb steeply to a crossroads, turn left and follow the sign to Cotswold Lavender. Pass the lavender farm and at the first Y-junction turn left, signed Broadway Tower. A couple of pleasant miles through woodland brings you to the tower and country park.

Built in 1799 by the Earl of Coventry as a focal point for his home – Croome Court in Worcestershire, about 15 miles to the north-west – Broadway Tower is a familiar landmark on the 1,024ft Broadway Hill above the village.

The 55ft mock-castle folly is one of England's finest viewpoints from where you can see 14 counties, including the Vales of Evesham and Gloucester and, on a clear day, the Welsh mountains.

Amazingly, a family lived in the windswept tower for forty years until the 1970s, with only a single springwater tap and a dozen persian cats for company.

Nearby, there's a memorial to the crew of an A.W. 38 Whitley bomber which crashed during a training mission in June 1943.

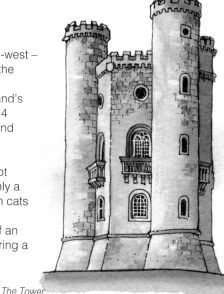

The Tower

❽ Broadway Tower

Folly Tower in an inspiring location. Large car park (fee payable), museum, deer park and a Morris & Brown café. There's also a genuine nuclear bunker on the site but sadly, considering the delicate state of the world, it's only open at weekends.

**Admission charge to roof views and bunker
Open daily 9am-5pm
Phone 01386 85239
www.broadwaytower.co.uk**

Rejoin the road you arrived on and turn left onto the A44. Descend winding Fish Hill to the roundabout entry into Broadway and the end of this tour.

The view from Broadway Country Park

Broadway

A large Cotswold showpiece village, Broadway has a wide main street edged with trim greens and a series of old stone 17th and 18th-century buildings, now housing a variety of gift shops, tea rooms, art galleries and antique dealers. Overlooked by the steep and wooded Cotswold edge and the folly of Broadway Tower, the village has something for everyone.

Situated on the main route between Oxford and Worcester, Broadway developed with the stagecoach trade and at one time had 23 inns, with seven coaches passing through every day. These days many more coaches call, but now they're luxury tourers carrying visitors from all over the world.

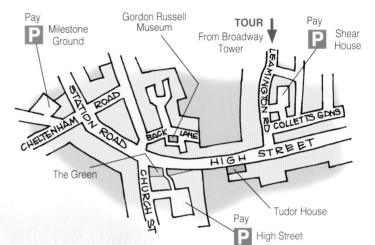

Shops in High Street

Double yellow lines deter parking on High Street, although there are a few laybys for short stops. Two of the three main car parks, High Street, off Church Street at the bottom end and Shear House off Leamington Road at the top are handily positioned for a stroll along one side of High Street and a return on the other.

The third park is a long stay off Station Road and involves a walk of around 600 yards to the bottom of High Street.

The west side of High Street

The large triangular green at the west end of High Street makes a picturesque start to a circuit up and down the street. Nearby is the grand, former coaching inn, The Lygon Arms, known to have been an inn since 1532, though it's possibly older. It was originally bought from General Lygon (who fought at Waterloo) by his butler, but it was developed into the world-renowned hotel of today by Sydney Bolton Russell. Both King Charles and Oliver Cromwell are reported to have stayed in the village – though probably not at the same time!

With the opening of the railway station in 1904, the coach trade began to decline and Broadway became one of the main stopping-off points for visitors exploring the Cotswolds. A stop on the old Great Western line, the station was closed in 1960 but after years of neglect a dedicated team of volunteers reopened the line in 2018 as part of the now 14-mile long heritage railway between Broadway and Cheltenham racecourse (See page 27).

John Noott Galleries

Broadway is said to have been 'discovered' by William Morris, the champion of the English Arts and Crafts movement, and the intellectuals of the 1890s. As an antidote to the bustle of High Street, duck down one of the signposted lanes which will take you to the Gordon Russell Museum, dedicated to the life and work of the acclaimed furniture designer (1892-1980). Russell came to Broadway at the age of twelve (when his father bought the Lygon Arms) and was influenced by the community of artists and craftsmen already active in the village. Following service as an officer in WWI he became a furniture designer. The museum showcases his life but the star attraction is the collection of wonderful Russell furniture.

Cottages in Upper High Street

The former St Michael's Church School at the top of High Street is dated 1856 and the projecting clock 1887. The school is now an art gallery.

Tudor House, a former 17th-century coaching inn stands next door and now houses the Ashmolean Museum Broadway. Spread over four floors, the objects on show are mostly on loan from the main museum in Oxford. Covering four hundred years of history up to the present day, exhibits include tapestries, furniture, ceramics and pottery, with paintings by Gainsborough and Reynolds, plus temporary exhibitions.

Beyond the Leamington Road junction you enter Upper High Street, a serene, mostly residential area, with a variety of fine old houses of weathered stone set in colourful gardens and backed by Broadway Hill. This could be the most beautiful built-up area in all of the north Cotswolds. Enjoy.

Food & Drink

As a major tourist attraction, Broadway boasts a huge variety of eateries, from fine dining to tea and cake. **Tisanes Tearoom** by the Green offers the full traditional, waitress-served tea and scones experience, while **The Bakehouse**, nearby, is licensed and serves artisan coffee. **Russell's** in High Street is well regarded with a classic English menu. For classy pub grub try the award-winning **Crown and Trumpet**, just behind the village green in Church Street.

The former St Michael's Church School and Tudor House

Chipping Norton to Stow-on-the-Wold · 23 miles

Beginning at the busy little town of Chipping Norton, this tour takes you into the 'the Oxfordshire Cotswolds', less busy than its Gloucestershire neighbour but with rolling landscapes crossed by ancient roads and dotted with ironstone villages, the area has much to like. Our first call is at the mysterious Rollright Stones with fantastic views, then on to Chastleton House, probably the most atmospheric of the many stately homes in the district.

Tiny Adlestrop is so quaint it has a world-famous poem written about it. After all the ancient attractions we take in ultra-modern Daylesford, where the rich and famous shop, then on to the delightful village of Kingham where they chill out. Bledington, just in Gloucestershire, is Cotswold perfection, before the tour ends at the tourist honeypot of Stow-on-the-Wold.

Chipping Norton – Little Compton – Chastleton – Adlestrop – Daylesford – Kingham – Churchill – Bledington – Stow-on-the-Wold

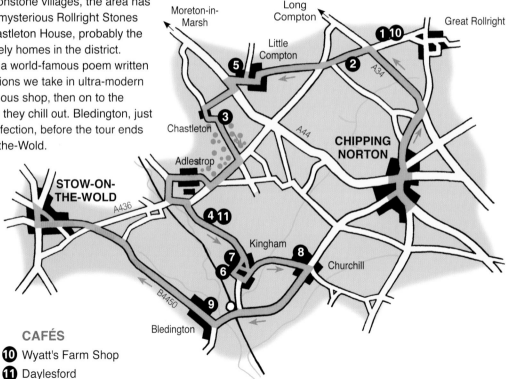

ATTRACTIONS
❶ Wyatt's Farm Shop
❷ Rollright Stones
❸ Chastleton House
❹ Daylesford

VILLAGE INNS
❺ Red Lion, Little Compton
❻ Wild Rabbit, Kingham
❼ Kingham Plough
❽ The Chequers, Churchill
❾ King's Head, Bledington

CAFÉS
❿ Wyatt's Farm Shop
⓫ Daylesford

Chipping Norton

The highest situated town in Oxfordshire and the most eastern outpost of the Cotswolds, Chipping Norton is situated on the western slopes of a hillside overlooking the Common Brook, a tributary of the River Evenlode.

'Chippy', as the bustling town in known locally, has never let tourism get in the way of everyday life and has 'proper' shops and an amiable air of normality not found in some of the usual Cotswold set pieces.

There's been a market here since the 13th century and during the 15th century the town was a major wool-trading centre. A terrace of impressive 17th to 19th-century hotels, inns and shops head the square, which is now mainly given over to parking, but a market is still held here on Wednesdays.

Built in 1842, the Palladian style Town Hall is a proud symbol of the days when the town was a borough. Apart from council business, which ended in 1857, the building has seen service as a lock-up, corn exchange and garage for the town fire engine. It's now used for corporate events and marriages.

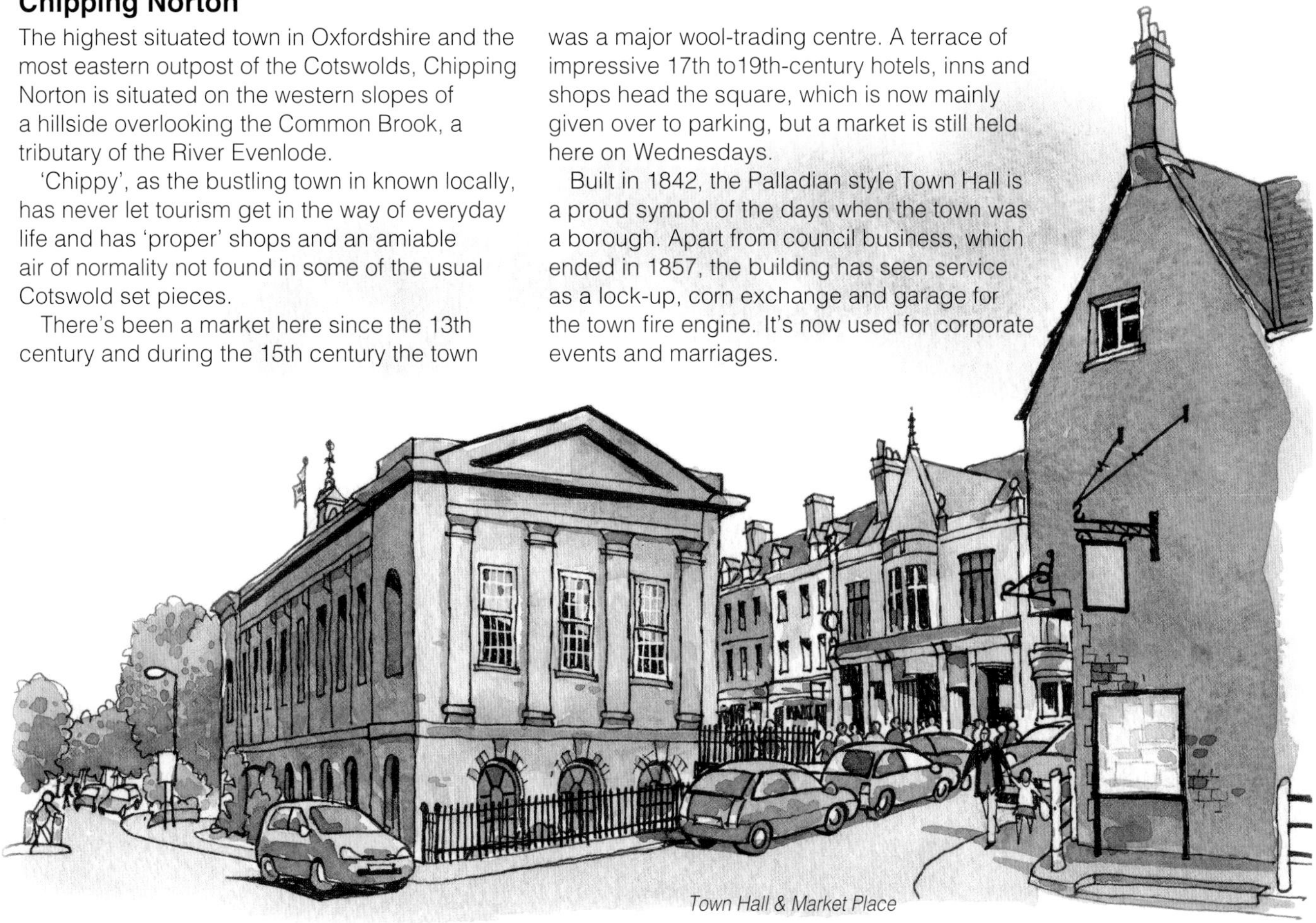

Town Hall & Market Place

39

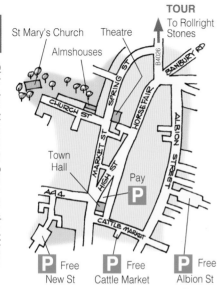

St Mary's Church   Theatre

Almshouses

TOUR
To Rollright
Stones

CHURCH ST
SPRING ST
MARKET ST
HIGH ST
HORSEFAIR
BANBURY RD
B4026
ALBION STREET

Town
Hall

Pay
P

A44

CATTLE MARKET

P Free
New St

P Free
Cattle Market

P Free
Albion St

The theatre

A walk along Market Street, takes you to the town's theatre, opened in 1975 by Tom Baker, who played Dr Who at the time. Once a Salvation Army citadel, the building is now a theatre, cinema, gallery and music venue, hosting original productions and touring companies.

Go down Church Street opposite where you pass a row of quaint, gabled almshouses (built in 1640), before arriving at the parish church.

A large, mostly Perpendicular building, St Mary's is one of the largest of the magnificent Cotswold churches financed by the proceeds of the medieval wool trade. The unusual hexagon porch (one of only three in England) has 15th-century stone vaulting incorporating a green man and various grotesque faces.

St Mary the Virgin Church

The sumptuous and lofty nave, rebuilt about 1450, is attributed to John Smyth, the designer of Eton College Chapel. There's also a splendid window above the chancel arch, with a rare inner veil of delicate stone tracery. Look out for the alabaster table-tombs commemorating 16th-century merchants Richard Croft and Thomas Richardes and their wives.

The Almshouses

The Blue Boar

Bliss Tweed Mill

Food & Drink

Fast food to high end places to eat and drink are plentiful around Market Square. The town isn't noted as a great 'foodie' destination but **Wild Thyme** in New Street is reckoned to be as classy as any in the area, serving modern British food with Mediterranean influences.

The **Blue Boar** is a beautiful traditional Cotswold pub. A listed building dating back to 1641, this old coach house is located at the end of High Street. A real local pub with a superb British seasonal menu, original wooden beams and a wood-burning stove.

Seek out a Chippy institution, **Jaffe and Neale**, an independent bookshop just off the main square. Packed with books, it also has an excellent little café where you can relax with coffee and cake after all that heavy browsing.

Situated on the western side of town, the Bliss Tweed Mill is Chipping Norton's most striking landmark, said to resemble a cross between a country mansion and a folly. It was built in 1872 and designed by George Woodhouse, a Lancashire architect. The building's dominant feature is its 165ft-high chimney stack rising from a ribbed leaded dome, which looks remarkably like a giant sink plunger.

The mill closed in the 1980s and was converted into 34 luxury apartments on five floors. William Bliss was instrumental in bringing the railway to Chipping Norton to supply coal for his mill's steam engines. The railway closed in the 1960s.

The Tour

Begin at the north end of Chipping Norton on the B4026 signed Over Norton. After about 1½ miles turn left at the junction with the A3400, signed Long Compton 3. After another 1½ miles turn left, signed Little Rollright 1½ & Little Compton. Climb gently to a broad ridge where there's a lay-by at the Rollright Stones.

Before turning left to the Stones you might fancy a short detour for coffee, turning right to Wyatts Farm Shop.

❷ Rollright Stones

This collection of megalithic monuments is scattered across the hillsides on both sides of the narrow road, which marks the Oxfordshire-Warwickshire border. The array consists of large natural stones moved here some three thousand years ago – nobody knows why – plus several burial chambers and burrows.

The main display, The King's Men, is on the south side of the road, consisting of seventy-seven limestones arranged in a circle of around a hundred feet in diameter. The large King's Stone is across the road with a number of scattered others.

Though not spectacular in the Stonehenge sense, the Rollright Stones are strangely atmospheric with terrific views from both sides of the road, but especially looking north across the Warwickshire countryside.

The view looking north

❶ Wyatts Farm Shop

Sells produce grown on the farm. The plant centre stocks hundreds of specialist trees, plants and roses. Tearoom with stunning views. They make their own famous ice cream and stage Fish & Chip Fridays, plus other events. Children's play area and garden.

Shop open Mon-Sat: 9am-5pm
Sun: 10am-4pm
Tearoom Mon-Sat: 9am-4.30pm
Sun: 10am-4pm
Phone 01608 684 835
www.wyattsgardencentre.co.uk

The King's Men

 From the Stones continue ahead for around half a mile, taking the second turning on your right into an unclassified road, signed Little Compton. Go through the village to the Red Lion Inn.

Little Compton

The Red Lion

5 Red Lion Inn

A well-regarded Donnington Brewery house serving above average pub fare. Two cosy double en-suite rooms available for B&B.

Bar open Mon-Sun: noon-11pm
Food Tue-Sat: noon-2.30pm & 6-9pm
Sun: noon-4pm
Kitchen closed on Mondays
Phone 01608 674397
www.theredlioninnlittlecompton.com

Set in a sheltered hollow between Barton Hill and the main Cotswold edge, this unassuming village – the most southern in Warwickshire – is a peaceful haven close to the busy A44. A stream flowing through the village is hailed as one of the tributaries of the mighty Thames. It flows west to join the Evenlode near Moreton-in-Marsh which flows into the Thames south of Oxford.

Thought to date to the 11th century, in 1644 the manor house became the home of William Juxon, then Bishop of London. Juxon had the unenviable task of attending King Charles I at his trial and subsequent execution. The bible used at the execution is on display at Chastleton House (see page 44) where Juxon regularly performed divine services. With the Rollright Stones, the manor was a film location for *Doctor Who's* 100th story, *The Stones of Blood*, and now houses the Reed Business School.

The 14th-century St Deny's Church next door to the manor has a stained glass window commemorating Juxon's role at the king's execution. It has a 14th-century tower and a saddleback roof, but the rest of the building dates from the 1860s and is generally considered to be of little interest to visitors.

Little Compton Manor

When you reach the junction with the A44 turn left signed Oxford and Chipping Norton. Turn right at the next junction, by the Old School, signed Chastleton village only. At the next T-junction turn left into a narrow road and climb past ancient farm buildings to Chastleton House.

43

Chastleton House

Built between 1607 and 1612 by Walter Jones, a prosperous Witney wool baron, this ranks as one of the most prestigious Jacobean houses in the country. The fascinating and atmospheric (some might say 'gloomy') interior has been largely undisturbed by any subsequent alteration since it was built. The National Trust took over the house in 1991 and restored the structure but wisely decided to retain the 'lived-in' look of the interior.

Its most outstanding features are the Long Gallery (72ft/22m long!) at the top of the house, where ladies took their winter exercise, and the Great Chamber, with its ceilings of ornate plasterwork. The house was used as one of the locations for the 2015 BBC Two television series *Wolf Hall*.

The dovecote

❸ Chastleton House

Splendid, ungentrified Jacobean country house. Free car park, but a 270-yard walk to the house. Return walk is up a steep hill. Outdoor footwear is recommended.

Admission charge
Open Apr-Sep. Wed-Sun: 1pm-5pm
Mar & Oct: Wed-Sun 1pm-4pm
www.nationaltrust.org.uk/ chastletonhouse

There's a topiary garden outside with medieval buildings nearby housing an exhibition about the house's restoration. The game of croquet began on lawns here with the rules of the game codified in 1865.

An arched dovecote in the field across the road, the site of a mansion demolished in the 19th century, bears the date 1762.

Continue past Castleton House car park and enter a woodland area. At the next crossroads turn right, along the A436, signed Adlestrop 1. Opposite the gates to a country estate turn right into a narrow unclassified road, signed Adlestrop ½. Park at the village hall near the bus shelter to explore the village on foot.

Adlestrop

'Quirky' perfectly describes this delightful small settlement, (population around 80). It's known internationally for an evocative poem written by Edward Thomas. Express trains once ran past the village but never stopped at the station. Then in 1914 one, 'unwontedly' did. The budding young poet was aboard and was so taken by the village name he began to write the now famous lines beginning 'Yes, I remember Adlestrop – the name...'.

The line survives but the station, a gem of Edwardian railway architecture, was closed in 1966 as part of the Beeching cuts. The station sign and a bench now stand in the bus shelter in the village as a poignant tribute to the young poet who was killed in action during WWI after immortalising the village he never saw. His poem is engraved on a brass plate on the bench.

Jane Austin used to visit her uncle Theophilus Leigh, who was rector in the village. The rectory (now Adlestrop House) stands next to the 13th-century church and the old school.

The bus shelter

Adlestrop still has a post office, a quirky stone, brick, timber and thatch building, although it's only open three days a week (Mon & Fri: 4pm –5pm, Thurs: 9.30am–5pm). There's also a modern racing stable near the village hall.

With its picturesque thatched cottages and olde world charm, Adlestrop is a delight to explore, but possibly its most quirky feature is that one of the cottages would fetch '£600,000 to a million-plus', according to a local estate agent.

Leave Adlestrop by turning right out of the car park opposite Adlestrop Stables to rejoin the main road. Turn left along the A436 for a short distance, signed Chipping Norton, then first right, signed Daylesford. The extensive estate is hidden from the road, but you can't miss the Daylesford Organic Farm shop.

Adlestrop post office

Daylesford & Kingham

Founded in the 1980s when local landowners the Bamford family converted their farming estates to organic, Daylesford Organic Farm has gathered a garland of awards and from some quarters a rather sniffy attitude to their relentless devotion to sustainability and healthy lifestyle in their high-end farm shop. Daylesford not only markets its own-brand products in Gloucestershire but also boasts three opulent outlets in London. It's a fascinating place to stop for a while and enjoy what the rich and famous consider as 'normal'.

Daylesford

The Wild Rabbit, Kingham

The Wild Rabbit at Kingham is an inn but not how mere mortals would know it. Run by Daylesford's organic food champion, Lady Angela Bamford, is has a bar at the front but beyond that, it's all luxuriance with plate glass, blond flagstones and darkwood furniture – all done in the best possible taste. It won Pub of the Year in 2015 so must be doing something right. But here the old pub lunch of a pint and a ploughman's is long gone.

④ Daylesford

Classy retail outlet of the Daylesford Organic Farm with premium deli items, butcher, fishmonger, garden shop, wellness spa, cookery school, café and restaurants. High end design and presentation with prices to match. Dubbed 'The Harvey Nichols of the Cotswolds'.

Open Mon-Sat: 8am-8pm
Sun: 10am-4pm
Tel: 01608 731700
www.daylesford.com

⑥ Wild Rabbit

Part of the Daylesford empire so you can be sure that the food, decor, rooms and rustic country inn charm are all overdone to perfection.

Open for food
Tue-Sat: noon-2.30pm & 7-9pm
Sun: noon-3pm
Tel: 01608 658389
www.thewildrabbit.co.uk

 From Daylesford continue to a Y-junction and turn right into Kingham. There's a car park at the top end of the green. A walk around the village is recommended.

Named 'England's favourite village' by a *Country Life* panel in 2004, Kingham is set splendidly on the Oxfordshire bank of the River Evenlode, a tributary of the Thames. With a large car park (free) at the top end of the spacious green, a walk down the main street of this friendly village is too good an invitation to miss.

Housed in an old limestone building, the much-praised Kingham Plough overlooks the green and an ancient well known as Stocks Well. Further along the attractive curving street, the village shop stands close to The Wild Rabbit, Kingham's other highly-rated hostelry.

❼ Kingham Plough

A Cotswold gastropub *par excellence.* Well-regarded for its daily-changing menu, service and seven county-style rooms.

Open for food
Mon-Thu: noon-9pm
Fri & Sat: noon-9.30pm
Sun: noon-3pm & 6-8pm
Tel: 01608 658327
www.thekinghamplough.co.uk

The Kingham Plough

The handsome former rectory at the end of the street dates from 1688. St Andrew's Church next door looks out across wonderful open countryside. A radical restoration by the Victorians in 1853 installed unusual stone ends and backs to the pews, the work of a local mason. There are also monuments to the Rev. William Dowdeswell, who built the rectory, and Lieutenant-Colonel Davis, depicting a soldier leaning on his tomb with a reversed rifle.

Leave Kingham at the NE corner, turning right into Churchill Road signed Churchill 2. In Churchill village turn right onto the B4450 at the T- junction signed Kingham Station & Sarsden. The Chequers pub is on your right and the magnificent tower of All Souls Church on your left.

Kingham Old Rectory

All Souls Church

Churchill & Bledington

The pleasant village of Churchill is strung out along the B4450 with the pinnacled tower of All Saints Church a landmark for miles around. Oddly, parts of the early 19th-century church are copies of various Oxford buildings. The nearby Memorial Fountain is even more bizarre – a folly in Victorian Gothic.

Warren Hastings (1732-1818), first Governor-General of British India was born in the village. On his return from India he bought back the family estates at nearby Daylesford, where he later died and was buried. Celebrity chef Rick Stein was also born in Churchill (in 1947).

The Chequers, Churchill

Bledington lies in the Evenlode valley on the Oxfordshire-Gloucestershire border. A large unfenced green at the village centre is crossed by a stream with a gaggle of resident noisy ducks. The 16th-century King's Head overlooks the green and is another of the Cotswolds' celebrated rural gastropub/hotels.

Set on rising land at the southern end of the green, the handsome parish church of St Leonard is well worth exploring. It dates from the 12th century and was much extended in the 15th.

To complete the rural idyll the green even has a maypole, erected in 1953 to replace one which dated back to 1887.

Mind the ducks!

Kings Head Inn, Bledington

8 Chequers

Welcoming gastropub at the heart of Churchill village. Local ales, traditional dishes, craft beers, scrubbed-wood tables and vintage ephemera.

Open daily noon-11pm
Tel: 01608 659393
www.thechequerschurchill.com

9 Kings Head

Good Pub Guide's Pub of the Year in 2018. Atmospheric furnishings, superb wines, real ales and delicious food. With 12 smart bedrooms it's the original cool Cotswold spot.

Food served Mon-Fri: noon-2pm &
6.30-9pm. Sat: noon-2.30pm
& 7-9pm
Tel: 01608 658365
www.thekingsheadinn.net

Keep on the B4450 and swing right opposite the church signed Kingham Station 2 & Bledington 3¼. Pass Kingham Station and soon after, the road turns sharp right into Bledington. Turn right across the green, signed B4450 Stow-on-the-Wold 4. Join the A436, turning left to the town and the end of this tour.

Stow-on-the-Wold

At 790ft above sea level, Stow is the highest situated town in the Cotswolds and, if legend is to be believed, the windiest. It's well placed at the junction of eight roads, one being the Roman Fosse Way. None of the main roads intrude on the remarkably large Market Square, leaving it largely traffic free for the multitude of visitors who flock to this engaging and historic small town.

The square was once a major sheep market with up to 20,000 animals sold in a day. In 1646, the town was the site of the last battle of the English Civil War. A royalist army, marching through the region in a desperate attempt to join the king at Oxford, was halted by parliamentary forces at Stow. The battle was messy with ducks reportedly swimming in blood flowing down Digbeth Street. Sir Jacob Astley sat on the base of the medieval cross in the square when he surrendered his Royalist Army to end the war.

Market Square

St Edward's House

Modern Stow is still centred on the square, with some decent shops and parking. A huge variety of inns and eating houses surround it, with narrow and twisting lanes going off to confine sheep, now lined with small independent shops.

St Edward's Hall was built in 1878, partly paid for by funds left unclaimed in the town's Savings Bank. The belfry tower was added in 1894 to house the fire bell, as the rector of the church wouldn't allow the church bell to be used. It's now the public library and a small museum.

The stocks in the Square

Use of the stocks, in which wrongdoers were once locked and exposed to public ridicule or assault, dates back to the 15th century, though it's doubtful if those in Stow Market Square have ever been used for real.

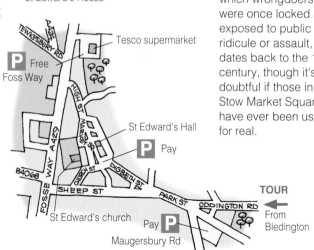

Tesco supermarket

P Free
Foss Way

St Edward's Hall

P Pay

TOUR ◀
From Bledington

St Edward's church

Pay **P**
Maugersbury Rd

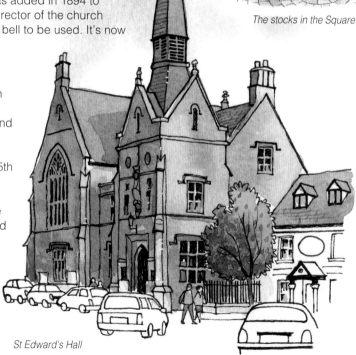

St Edward's Hall

King's Arms

St Edward's House, at the top of the square, looks ancient with its worn stonework and twin fluted Corinthian pilasters, but was actually built in the early 18th century.

The picturesque King's Arms was a flourishing coaching inn as early as 1647, with a reputation as the best between London and Worcester. Charles I famously stayed here before the Battle of Naseby in 1645 and it was the location for the BBC's TV adaption of the Thomas Hardy novel, *The Mayor of Casterbridge*.

Dating to Norman and tudor times, St Edward's Church suffered extensive damage while housing 1,000 royalist prisoners at the end of the English Civil War.

The local wool trade funded various restorations and the large Cotswold stone building was largely restored by the end of the 1800s. The 88ft-high Perpendicular tower, built during the 15th century, boasts the heaviest peel of bells in Gloucestershire. In the south aisle there's a large painting of the Crucifixion by Gaspar de Craeyer (1582-1669), a contemporary of Reubens and Van Dyck.

Seek out the north doorway where two yew trees flanking the old wooden door appear to have become part of the stonework.

St Edward's Church

Food & Drink

Huffkins in the square is a legendry Cotswold tearoom noted for its afternoon teas, but also good for snacks and light meals.

Coach House Coffee is on two floors and overlooks the square, a good place to people watch while you're savouring Gluten and dairy-free cakes and produce.

The Porch House at the bottom of Digbeth Street is billed as 'England's oldest Inn'. Dating back to 947AD, the building has had various uses over the years and was only converted to a restaurant and hotel in 1970. Modern and fairly posh with a cosy dining area.

For something different try the **In the Mood Tearoom,** located in the narrow part of Digbeth Street and 1940s themed. Enjoy a coffee or loose leaf tea while sashaying to big band music. They also serve hot meals and high teas.

Stow-on-the-Wold to Bourton-on-the-Water · 22 miles

Stow-on-the-Wold – Upper Swell – Lower Swell –
Cotswold Farm Park – Ford – Temple Guiting – Kineton –
Guiting Power – Naunton – Upper Slaughter – Lower
Slaughter – Bourton-on-the-Water

ATTRACTIONS

1 Cotswold Farm Park
2 Old Mill, Lower Slaughter

VILLAGE INNS

3 Golden Ball, Lower Swell
4 Plough Inn, Ford
5 Halfway House, Kineton
6 Miners Arms, Guiting Power
7 Hollow Bottom, Guiting Power
8 Black Horse, Naunton

CAFÉS

9 Cotswold Farm Park
10 Guiting Power
11 Temple Guiting
12 Old Mill, Lower Slaughter

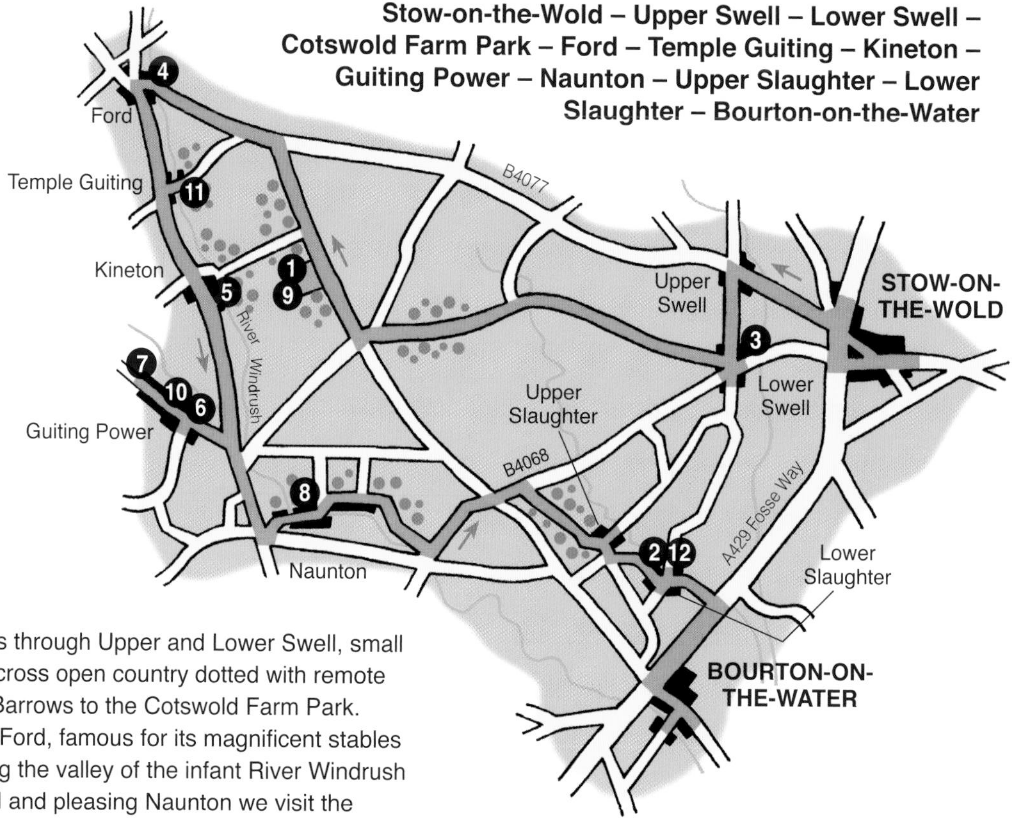

From Stow-on-the-Wold this tour goes through Upper and Lower Swell, small
villages on the River Dikler. We then cross open country dotted with remote
farms, disused quarries and ancient Barrows to the Cotswold Farm Park.
Turning north the route goes through Ford, famous for its magnificent stables
and racing pub, then turns south along the valley of the infant River Windrush
to three varied villages. After peaceful and pleasing Naunton we visit the
delightful Slaughters, possibly the two most visited villages in the area, with the
tour ending at pretty Bourton-on-the-Water, also hugely popular.

The Tour

Leave Stow on the B4077 at the north end of the village signed Upper Swell and Cotswold Farm Park. After a mile or so cross a bridge over the River Dikler into Upper Swell. The Old Mill is on your right. Continue up the hill along an avenue of trees. At the top of the hill as you leave the village, turn left onto a narrow minor road signed Lower Swell and The Golden Ball Inn.

This climbs steadily for some fine views across the countryside. Continue past St Mary's Church to the centre of Lower Swell where it's usually possible to park around the village green.

The Mill

Upper Swell

This quiet, hamlet of pretty and affluent Cotswold stone houses spreads down a deeply wooded hill to the River Dikler, where a three-arched 18th-century bridge carries traffic on the B4077 road to Stow. An early 19th-century mill with its waterwheel intact stands by the bridge, from where you can see a moss-covered weir and the large mill pond beyond. A row of attractive 18th-century houses are attached to the mill. Parking in Upper Swell is difficult and there are no amenities.

Further upstream the Dikler has been damned to drive a large waterwheel at Donnington Brewery. The company's ales have been on sale throughout the Cotswolds since 1865 and the brewery now supplies its own 15 tied houses and a number of local free houses with quality 'real ale'.

The single road through the village

The village green

③ Golden Ball Inn

A traditional family-run village pub serving
Donnington Ales and locally sourced food.

Opening Times:
Bar Mon-Fri: noon-3pm & 5-11pm
Sat & Sun: noon -11pm
Food Mon-Sat: 12.30-2pm & 6.30-9pm
Sun: 12.30-3pm
Phone 01451 833886
www.thegoldenballinn.com

Lower Swell

Situated on the banks of the River Dikler on the busy B4068, once the
main Stow to Cheltenham road, the tidy village of Lower Swell gathers
around a triangular green near the village hall. Most of the buildings,
even the new ones, are of stone and many have Cotswold stone roofs.
The oldest surviving houses are 17th century, including the well-
regarded Golden Ball Inn.

The Dikler flows through the park of Abbotswood, a fine early
20th- century mansion built by Sir Edwin Lutyens, and at one time the
home of inventor and tractor millionaire, Harry Ferguson. Lutyens also
designed the war memorial on the village green.

St Mary's Church has 12th-century origins with some remarkable
Norman carvings, particularly on the doorway and chancel arch. The
building was altered in the 15th century and greatly enlarged in 1852,
so the original Norman church now serves as
the south aisle.

Golden Ball Inn

There are usually places to park with
consideration around the green but, apart from
the inn, the village has no other visitor facilities.

*Leave on the road to the west of the green, signed Guiting Power 6.
Climb steadily on the straight road across flat farmland with extensive
views, occasional farm buildings and possibly geese in the road. After around four
miles you arrive at a crossroads of minor roads. Turn right, signed Snowshill. The
entrance to Cotswold Farm Park is a half mile further on.*

Joe Henson founded the Cotswold Farm Park in 1971 to help protect rare breeds of farm animals. His son Adam and business partner Duncan have carried on his work and now visitors can meet over 50 flocks and herds of rare farm animals, including Gloucestershire Old Spot pigs and Highland cattle.

Apart from being a good day out for families, the park serves as a reminder that though tourism is vital to the Cotswold economy, farming is still its backbone.

Cotswold Farm Park visitor tour 'bus'

 Continue to the B4077 then turn left amongst trees, signed Ford 1¼. Pass Oathill Quarry. As you enter the hamlet of Ford look right for the white rails of the gallops of Grand National and Cheltenham Gold Cup winning trainer Jonjo O'Neil's state-of-the-art racing stables estate, Jackdaws Castle.

Plough Inn

❶ Cotswold Farm Park

BBC TV *Countryfile* star Adam Henson's survival centre for rare historic breeds of British farm animals set high on the Cotswold hills. Pets and tots corners. Farm trail. Lambing, shearing, seasonal exhibitions and demonstrations. Café. Camping. Open daily February to December.

Admission charge
Phone 01451 850307
www.cotswoldfarmpark.co.uk

❹ Plough Inn, Ford

Famous 16th-century racing pub. Georgian-style restaurant and three en-suite rooms overlooking the gallops. Winner of Cotswold Food & Drink 'Cotswold Best Pub Award 2017' and Racing Pub of the Year in 2008. Hugely popular. Book early for Cheltenham race week.

Pub & dining times
Mon-Thu: noon-2.15pm &
6-9.15pm
Fri-Sun: noon-9.15pm
(bar open all day)
School holidays
noon-9.15pm (bar open all day)
Phone 01386 584215
www.theploughinnford.co.uk

Go down the hill through Ford to cross the infant River Windrush. Climb through trees and, as they clear, turn sharp left onto a narrow road signed Temple Guiting 1¼. There's a lovely little shop and tea room at the village centre that requires some patience to find.

Turn left opposite the school and keep following the heavily wooded road as it twists and turns. Look out for a small notice board on the right-hand roadside that marks the village centre. Turn right here signed 'Post Office & Village Shop'.

Main street, Ford

Ford & Temple Guiting

Ford is a pretty hamlet on the open slopes of the upper Windrush valley, while Temple Guiting is secreted away in woodland further downstream. There are deep pools above and below a small bridge over the river.

Temple Guiting is an ancient site, owned by the Knights Templars around 1150 when they worked a fulling mill at nearby Barton. The village name has extended their influence over the centuries since.

Village shop, Temple Guiting

⑤ Halfway House

A 17th-century inn, owned by Corpus Christi College of Oxford University until 1975 and now a relaxed village pub with good traditional food using local ingredients. Children and dogs are welcome and there's a pretty, sheltered back garden.

Open Mon-Thu: noon-10 pm
Fri & Sat: noon-11pm. Sun: noon to 9pm
Food served: noon-8.45pm daily
Tel: 01451 850344
www.thehalfwayhousekineton.co.uk

Halfway House, Kineton

Return to the school and turn left along the road you were following previously. Go through the hamlet of Kineton where there's a pub, The Halfway House. A further mile or so brings you to the entrance to a large private estate. Turn right down the road opposite signed Guiting Power ¼. With two pubs and a post office Guiting Power begs be explored on foot. You can park at the village hall.

Guiting Power

Situated on the slopes of a small valley formed by a tributary of the River Windrush, Guiting Power is unusual for its size in having a post office, village hall and two pubs. The mellow stone houses cluster around a sloping village green with 1918 War Memorial Cross of medieval design at its centre. The village hosts the Guiting Festival for ten days each July, with top folk, jazz and classical artists performing in the village hall.

The Guiting Manor Amenity Trust, founded by the Lord of the Manor, Raymond Cochrane in the early 1970s, protects the village from an influx of second-home buyers.

The parish church of St Michael stands rather isolated in fields at the south end of the village. Of Norman origins, the building was remodelled over the centuries and enlarged in the 1800s during a severe Victorian renovation. The Norman north and south doorways survived and make a visit worthwhile.

❻ Farmer's Arms

A nicely old-fashioned village pub with stripped stone, flagstones and a woodburner. Skittle alley, darts, dominoes, cribbage and pool. Serves Donnington beer and traditional home-cooked food, including rabbit pie.

Open Tue-Sun: 11.30am-3pm & 5.30-11pm
Closed Mondays
Tel: 01451 850358
www.donnington-brewery.com

❼ Hollow Bottom

Traditional 17th-century inn with five letting rooms. Busy, friendly atmosphere with a regular clientele of racing folk from the local stables. Decent beer and excellent food.

Open all day, every day 9am-11.45pm
Three sittings for their famous Sunday roasts: noon, 2pm and 3.30pm
Tel: 01451 850392
www.hollowbottom.com

Post office

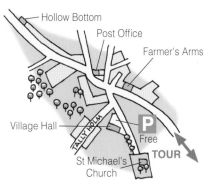

Hollow Bottom

Post Office

Farmer's Arms

TALLY HOLM

Village Hall

P Free

TOUR

St Michael's Church

Hollow Bottom

Return along the village road to the estate gates and turn right along the road you left earlier. Ignore the sign pointing left to Naunton and keep straight on, climbing through woodland for some extensive views. Descend to the Foxhill B&B and turn left onto the B4068. A quarter of a mile later, fork left at Church Farm, signed Naunton ¼.

Naunton

A long and narrow village, Naunton is strung out along the River Windrush in an almost continuous cavalcade of Cotswold perfection. Seen from the hills above, the village and church look like a model in an estate agent's window.

A now famous dovecote incorporating four gables around a central turret was erected in 1660 near the bridge over the river.

Naunton's Church of St Andrew has a handsome Perpendicular tower with pinnacles, gargoyles and a restored ring of six bells. Two sundials on the tower date from the 18th century. There has been a church on this site since Saxon times, and a cross from that time survives in the wall. Although the interior was much changed at the end of the Victorian era, the present building is still largely 15th century with a beautifully carved stone pulpit and font from that period.

❽ Black Horse

Serving ale since the 1870's, the Black Horse was originally sold to The Stow Brewery in 1896 for £570. Now its one of Donnington Brewery's 15 pub outlets. The bar still has its original flagstone floors and a welcoming fire during the winter, plus a warm welcome from one of the pub's friendly dogs. Wide range of pub grub from sandwiches to more substantial meals.

Opening times
Mon-Thu: 11am-3pm & 6-11.30pm
Fri-Sat: 11am-11.30pm
Sun: noon-11-30pm
Tel: 01451 850565
www.theblackhorsenaunton.co.uk

Naunton gable ends

Black Horse

The Square and St Peter's Church

Keep on Naunton village road to rejoin the B4068, turning left signed Stow. About half a mile beyond Brockhill Quarry turn right onto a narrow road signed The Slaughters. Turn left at the Upper Slaughter sign. Parking is limited to the main square but it's well worth stopping if you can find a space.

Upper Slaughter

This lovely village is situated on the little River eye, less than two miles from its source below Eyford Hill. It's less visited than its celebrity neighbour, Lower Slaughter, but is equally delightful.

The ford on the River Eye

Warm Cotswold stone cottages, re-modelled by Lutyens in 1906, grouped around a small square look picturesque enough, but the lane that rises past Upper Slaughter church unexpectedly dips into a scene of blissful Englishness.

A ford crosses the gentle River Eye (known locally as Slaughter Brook) beneath a single, magnificent sycamore tree. To the left, across an acre of mown grass, stands the gabled Manor House, one of the finest examples of Elizabethan domestic architecture in the Cotswolds. Little stone bridges cross the river, fringed by wildflowers and rushes. This is a special place.

St Peter's Church

The pinnacled tower of St Peter's Church is an attractive feature on the hilltop above the river. Originally Norman, the building was largely rebuilt in 1877 and the interior is clearly Victorian with a grand memorial to F.E. Witts, the local rector and lord of the manor, who died in 1854. A brass commemorates John Slaughter (1583) whose family built the Manor House in the 16th century.

Far from its brutal connotation, 'Slaughter' is possibly derived from an Old English word meaning 'slough' or 'boggy place'.

One of the slab bridges over the river

Apart from somewhere to park (and the scenery), the village has no amenities for casual visitors.

Return along the road you turned off to the village and turn left, signed Lower Slaughter. Parking is even more difficult here with double yellow lines all over the place. Best (only) bet is to park on the side of Copsehill Road. An alternative is to park in Upper Slaughter and walk along the wonderful Warden's Way, which follows the River Eye for around a mile to the mill at Lower Slaughter.

Lower Slaughter

The epitome of Cotswold charm, with a string of immaculate stone houses winding along the banks of leisurely River Eye, crossed by a series of delightful small bridges and overhung at the east end by graceful willows. Thankfully for the visitor, the small, trim village has been able to resist most over-commercialisation of its many attractions.

The owner of the quarry at Little Barrington, Valentine Strong, built Lower Slaughter Manor House during the 1650's. The Manor is now a luxury hotel and a popular venue for society and show-biz weddings.

St Mary's Church next door has an impressive spire and blends in well with the old houses, although it's a largely Victorian rebuild. Some of the original 13th-century arches have been retained and there's pretty stained glass windows on three sides of the building.

The Old Mill and millwheel

The photographer's favourite view

❷ Old Mill

Milling ended here in 1958 after over 800 years of production and the mill reopened as a museum in 1995. Part of the building was for a time the village post office and shop.

Now run by jazz singer and crooner, Gerald Harris, it's become an amazing Aladdin's cave of unusual quality items to buy while accompanied by music from the Great American Songbook.

You can unwind on the mill's café terrace overlooking the river and enjoy 'simple dishes lovingly prepared from the best local produce'.

Open daily
1st Mar to 31st Oct 10am-6pm
1st Nov to 28th Feb 10am until dusk
Tea room and café terrace close at 5pm
Entrance fee to museum
Shop tel: 01451 822127
River Café: 01451 850392
Office: 01451 820052
www.oldmill-lowerslaughter.com

Doorway overlooking the river

With some of the most celebrated village scenery in the Cotswolds, Lower Slaughter attracts many visitors. Try to time your tour to arrive here around mid afternoon when the day trippers have left and there's a possibility of finding somewhere to park.

The Old Mill can provide refreshment but if you have deep pockets you could try one of the grand hotels in the village. The Slaughters Country Inn is more approachable than most and is notably family friendly.

Leave the village along Copsehill Road to the A429. Turn right, signed Cirencester, passing the Coach & Horses, to traffic lights where you turn left into Station Road to enter Bourton-on-the-Water. To avoid having to drive along busy High Street, stay on Station Road to the car parks and the end of this tour.

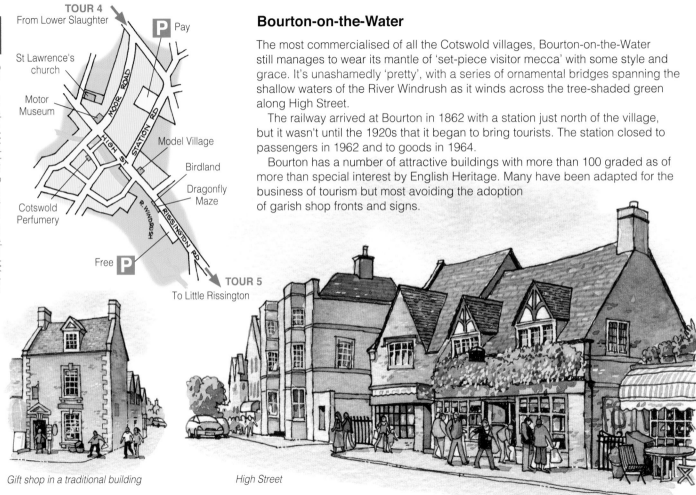

TOUR 4
From Lower Slaughter

P Pay

St Lawrence's church

Motor Museum

HIGH ST

MOOR ROAD

STATION RD

Model Village

Birdland

Dragonfly Maze

Cotswold Perfumery

R. WINDRUSH

RISSINGTON RD

Free P

TOUR 5
To Little Rissington

Bourton-on-the-Water

The most commercialised of all the Cotswold villages, Bourton-on-the-Water still manages to wear its mantle of 'set-piece visitor mecca' with some style and grace. It's unashamedly 'pretty', with a series of ornamental bridges spanning the shallow waters of the River Windrush as it winds across the tree-shaded green along High Street.

The railway arrived at Bourton in 1862 with a station just north of the village, but it wasn't until the 1920s that it began to bring tourists. The station closed to passengers in 1962 and to goods in 1964.

Bourton has a number of attractive buildings with more than 100 graded as of more than special interest by English Heritage. Many have been adapted for the business of tourism but most avoiding the adoption of garish shop fronts and signs.

Gift shop in a traditional building

High Street

Motor Museum

Bourton has a number of well-established visitor attractions:

The **Motor Museum** is housed in an old watermill at the northern end of the green. Though its main focus is on motoring, the museum is packed with the everyday paraphernalia that made motoring such a pleasure, including picnic sets from the 1920s, caravans, radio sets – and knitted swimsuits!

The **Model Village** is sited in the garden of the Old New Inn and is a perfect one-ninth miniature in stone of Bourton itself. It was built by an earlier inn-owner with a small team of local craftsmen and opened in1937. The Model Village includes a model of itself with its own miniature Windrush, around ten centimetres wide, running through it.

Located on the outskirts of the village in a former trout farm on the Windrush, **Birdland** is home to over 500 birds, including penguins, flamingoes and pelicans.

The **Dragonfly Maze** nearby is a yew maze with a pavilion at the centre.The object is not only to reach the pavilion, but to gather clues as you navigate the maze. Correctly interpreting the clues when you reach the pavilion provides access to the maze's final secret.

Cotswold Perfumery in Victoria Street, one of Europe's few manufacturers and retailers of perfume, can be an unexpected pleasure with a shop, informative factory tours and one-day courses on how to create your own fragrance.

St Lawrence's Church

Feeding the ducks on the Windrush

Built on earlier Saxon foundations, St Lawrence's Church has a 14th-century chancel, which was retained when the building was rebuilt in 1784 by William Marshall, who lived in the village.

He also designed the eccentric three stage tower, rusticated at the base with enormous Ionic pilasters, cornices and balustrades and topped with a lead-covered dome. Two clocks on the south face only add to the confused design.

The church underwent further rebuilding between the years 1875-90, this time by a more competent architect, Sir Thomas Jackson. He kept the chancel and tower, building on to them a new five-bay nave and a north isle. Despite attractive pointed arches and round piers, the interior remains Victorian in character and rather gloomy.

Bourton's bridges and the canal-like look of the Windrush have led to the village being tagged, somewhat fancifully, the 'Venice of the Cotswolds'. However, the five bridges in the main village are delightful and some are surprisingly old.

Mill Bridge, a road bridge at the western end of the village, was built in 1654, replacing a ford and originally called Broad or Big Bridge.

High Bridge, a footbridge at the centre of the green, dates back to 1756.

Payne Bridge is another foot bridge, dated 1776.

New Bridge was built in 1911 by a local benefactor, George Frederick Moore, a successful tea-planter who did much to enhance the appearance of the green.

Coronation Bridge, opposite the Old New Inn, was built in 1953, replacing an earlier wooden structure dating back to 1750.

The Windrush is one of Bourton's most cherished features. Fish dart through the clear water and a gaggle of ducks is always on hand to delight the children.

Mill Bridge

High Bridge

Payne Bridge

New Bridge

Coronation Bridge

Food & Drink

Almost every other building in Bourton's High Street seems to house a tea shop, restaurant or hotel. You won't go hungry or thirsty here.

The Duke of Wellington is a large Elizabethan village inn on the corner of Sherbourne Street offering a large range of dishes. Family and vegetarian friendly.

For the full English breakfast, morning coffee, afternoon tea and dinner experience, try **Croft** in Victoria Street, **Rose Tree Restaurant** on the Green, **Smiths of Bourbon** in Victoria Street and **Chestnut Tree Tea Room** in High Street. All have favourable reviews.

Bourton-on-the-Water to Burford · 23 miles

Bourton-on-the-Water – Little Rissington – Great Rissington – Great Barrington –
Little Barrington – Sherborne – Windrush – Great Barrington – Tayton – Burford

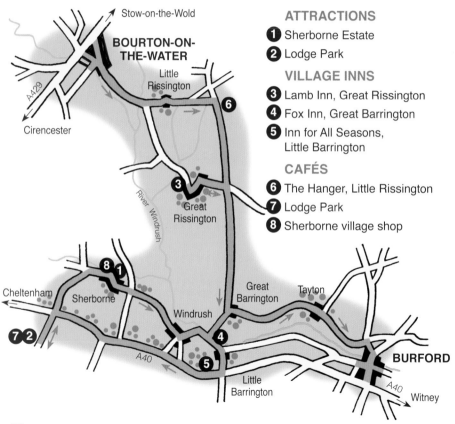

ATTRACTIONS
1 Sherborne Estate
2 Lodge Park

VILLAGE INNS
3 Lamb Inn, Great Rissington
4 Fox Inn, Great Barrington
5 Inn for All Seasons,
   Little Barrington

CAFÉS
6 The Hanger, Little Rissington
7 Lodge Park
8 Sherborne village shop

This route generally follows the River Windrush on its journey south from Bourton-on-the-Water to Burford. We pass the former World War II air base on the high flatlands at Little Rissington before descending to the hillside village of Great Rissington overlooking the Windrush valley.

Heading south we go through the estate village of Great Barrington and cross the river to the popular Fox Inn. A climb through picturesque Little Barrington, set around a disused quarry, takes us to the A40 and the handsome Inn for All Seasons.

A short diversion takes in the 17th-century grandstand at Lodge Park, once the playground of the aristocracy and now part of Sherborne Estate. We continue through Sherborne village, long and scattered, with access to walks across the country park.

On to Windrush, a village as pretty as its name, with Cotswolds' cottages worthy of many a calendar, plus a historic church. Through tiny Taynton, also picture-perfect, we join the A361 to cross the river and the conclusion of this tour at Burford.

The Tour

Leave Bourton-on-Water on the Rissington road, passing Birdland to Little Rissington, a small and peaceful place but plain by Cotswold standards. With a windswept and open aspect it's set in farming country overlooking several flooded gravel pits, some now nature reserves. The graves of young men killed during World War II while flying from the nearby airfield on the hill can be found in the neat churchyard.

Turn right at the next tee junction at Upper Rissington, signed Great Rissington and The Lamb Inn. The road avoids Upper Rissington, one of the highest villages in the Cotswolds, and passes Little Rissington Airport, once the location of the Central Flying School and home of the Red Arrows aerial display team until being closed in the 1970s. The northern end is now a business park with an American style café, The Hanger.

Beyond the airfield turn right onto an unclassified road, signed Great Rissingdon 5. Pass an impressive sports club and playing field before descending to the village green, where the Lamb Inn is on your right.

Great Rissington

Despite its name, Great Rissington is a modest sized village which faces westwards across the broad Windrush Valley. It's the southernmost of the three Cotswold Rissingtons and grouped around a sloping triangular green at its north west corner.

The old houses are of weathered Cotswold stone with the most notable buildings – church, manor house and rectory – located at the far southwest corner.

6 The Hanger

American style diner and bar.

**Open for food: Mon-Fri 7am-3pm
Sat 9am-4pm. Sun closed
Phone 01451 821107
www.thehangeruk.co.uk**

Cottages overlooking the green

You can usually park with consideration around the green from where a leisurely stroll down the main street to the church is highly recommended.

You can return along one of the tangle of lanes which weave around this delightful village.

St John's Church

❸ Lamb Inn

A large and attractively rambling building of mellow Cotswold stone with some parts over 300 years old. This is a thriving country pub with great food, a sunny garden, and rural peace and quiet. There are twelve comfortable guest rooms.

Bar open daily 11.30am–11pm
Food served:
Mon-Fri: noon-2:30pm Sat & Sun: noon-3pm
Sun-Thu 6.30-9pm. Fri & Sat: 6.30-9.30pm
Tel: 01451 820388
www.thelambinn.com

Attractively situated between the manor house and a Georgian rectory (now a private house), St John the Baptist Church is set on a small rise.

The oldest parts of the cruciform building date from the 12th century, while the square central tower, ornamented with battlements and pinnacles, is 15th century. The 12th-century nave arch leads to a square area under the tower, where the column capitals are beautifully carved with ornamental leaves. Don't miss the striking memorial to John Barnarde (d.1621) on the east wall and the 15th-century carving of the Crucifixion in the porch

Originally a 17th-century farmhouse, the manor house and park have been extensively extended since.

Lamb Inn

Resume driving and climb back up the hill past the sports ground and turn right, signed The Barringtons. The small hamlet of Great Barrington is largely the private Barrington Park Estate, so it's hardly worth stopping. Instead turn right, signed Little Barrington, and cross a stone bridge built by local master-mason Thomas Strong over the River Windrush, to the Fox Inn.

❹ Fox Inn

A traditional riverside Inn and restaurant with rustic soul by the bucket load. Stunning views, award-winning dining, a proper bar and seven handsome bedrooms. A cosy hostelry for locals and Cotswold explorers.

Pub Open: All day, everyday!
Open for food:
Mon-Fri: noon-2.30pm & 6.30-9.30pm
Sat & Sun: noon-9.30pm
Tel: 01451 844385
www.foxinnbarrington.com

Fox Inn

Continue left to Little Barrington, a gathering of stone Cotswold houses and terraces attractively grouped around a sloping bowl-shaped green, originally a quarry. Climb the hill to the A40 and turn right, signed The Inn for All Seasons, which you soon come to on your right. Now an upmarket hotel, it was allegedly built to slake the thirst of the numerous quarrymen who once worked in the area.

Little Barrington

Inn for All Seasons

Keep on the A40 for about 2½ miles to reach a crossroads where the road to the right is signed Sherborne, but first turn left down a narrow straight road opposite signed Lodge Park (NT). After your visit return to the A40 and cross into the road opposite signed Sherborne.

The Grandstand

Lodge Park is part of the Sherborne Estate which includes the village we will visit later. It's main feature is a unique 17th-century grandstand, built by John 'Crump' Dutton. Looking more like a beautiful little house than a modern grandstand, the Lodge originally had guest rooms but was primarily built for the contemporary pastimes of rich aristocrats: feasting, gambling and watching the coursing of deer by greyhounds. You can climb to the roof and admire the parkland redesigned by renowned landscape designer Charles Bridgeman in 1726.

❺ Inn for All Seasons

A 16th-century coaching inn providing every modern convenience, while retaining much of the character and style of a quintessential Cotswolds inn. Originally the Barrington New Inn, the name was changed in the 1960s by owner Jeremy Taylor as homage to his previous career as a horse master working on films including *Lawrence of Arabia*, *A Winters Tale* and *The Man for all Seasons*. There's ten comfortable, en suite letting bedrooms, exposed beams, flagstone floors, Cotswold stone walls, large fireplaces and a beautiful garden.

Breakfast 8am-11am
Food served all day, last orders 8.45pm
The bar is open if there are customers, otherwise it closes at 10pm
Tel: 01451 844324
www.innforallseasons.com

❷ Lodge Park

Parkland and picturesque grandstand. Refreshments, cakes and ice-creams available. Picnic in the park. Dogs welcome in the park.

Admission charge
Open: Fridays, Saturdays and Sundays from Mar-Oct
www.nationaltrust.org.uk/lodgepark

Sherborne

Built of grey-stone along Sherborne Brook, a tributary of the Windrush, Sherborne village is part of the Sherborne House Estate situated on the valley road between Burford and Northleach.

Winchcombe Abbey owned the estate during the middle ages. The Dutton family acquired it in 1551 and by 1651 had built Sherborne House. After a period as a boarding school, the family bequeathed the estate to the National Trust in the 1980s and the house has been divided into luxury flats. The land is now a large park, open to the public with walks, old farm buildings and a sculpture trail.

Sherborne Estate

A working Cotswold estate, a place of quiet walks and abundant wildlife. Eighteenth-century water meadows home to otters, water voles and dragonflies, with sculptures and a play area. Park at Water Meadows car park along the road going north from the eastern end of the village. Dogs welcome. Free entry.

www.nationaltrust.org.uk/sherborne-park

Sherborne is an exceptionally long village, extending for over a mile in a series of winding undulations along a single road, with the east and west ends separated by Sherborne Park. You can usually park at the centre near the village shop and school (but avoid pick-up times!). Apart from the shop, which serves refreshments, the village has no other facilities.

St Mary Magdalene Church dates from the 14th century but the present building was largely built in the 17th or later. The lofty interior is largely a mausoleum to the Dutton family, whose lavish monuments dominate the chancel.

A roadside cottage at the east end of the village has a 12th-century doorway with a carved tympanum, which could mean it was once a church or (more likely) the stone may have come from a demolished Norman church.

Shop & post office

Sherborne House

Keep on the road through Sherborne to Windrush, another place worth having a look round. Park as close to the church as possible, where there's a small green and much to admire.

Approaching Windrush

Windrush

The Windrush is the largest of the Cotswold rivers and the delightful village, which takes its name clings to the steep slopes above its lush water meadows. The main part of the small settlement is gathered around a tiny village green overlooked by a number of attractive stone houses and cottages, with an avenue of lime trees leading off to the church.

The lanes going out of the village are worth exploring and there are some excellent walks along the river, upstream to Sherborne or downstream to Little Barrington.

Windrush was once noted for the quality of its stone, white oolite, hewn from mines up to a quarter of a mile in length, driven into the hillsides between the village and the present A40. In 1839 a Royal Commission chose Windrush stone for the renovation of parts of the Houses of Parliament.

When stringent new health and safety regulations were introduced it became difficult for the business to continue profitably, and by 1900 the mines had closed.

Many of the idyllic houses in the old quarrying village are built from the local stone. Some date to the 17th century and one has a date stone of 1668.

Windrush village

St Peter's Church

During World War II an RAF station was based near the village. A memorial stone in the churchyard wall commemorates Sgt Pilot Bruce Hancock RAFVR, who gave his life by ramming and destroying an enemy bomber while flying an unarmed training aircraft during the Battle of Britain in 1940.

Following closure in 1945, the airfield was used by a local flying club and for parachuting until 1997. The control tower has been preserved.

The south doorway

The Church of St Peter commands the highest ground with a handsome perpendicular tower. The churchyard boasts a remarkable collection of tombs, mainly 18th century, which consists of variations of the table design. One dated 1713 has a roll top with a ram's head set into its scalloped end. They seem unexpectedly extravagant in this tranquil setting, but the Norman south doorway is even more fantastic. A double row of grotesque beak-headed demons with strange staring eyes warn the worshipper that he who hesitates in crossing the portal is lost. In one of the finest collections in the Cotswolds, each stone head is subtly different from its neighbour and considering their exposed position they are in remarkable condition.

Inside, St Peter's is comparatively plain, having suffered a drastic restoration in 1874, but there's still a lovely 15th-century roof to the nave, medieval floor tiles and a Jacobean pulpit to admire.

Continue down the hill out of Windrush and turn left past the Fox Inn, retracing your earlier route. Go through Great Barrington to the small village of Taynton. Beyond Taynton turn right to join the A361 and cross the bridge into Burford High Street, the end of this tour.

Taynton

Trim and compact, the stone-built village of Taynton is a collection of classic Cotswold farms, houses and terraced cottages, some thatched. The ancient settlement is only just in Oxfordshire with the Gloucestershire county border just a few fields away to the west. The River Windrush twists and turns between willow trees to the south.

Taynton stone has been quarried here since early medieval times. Cotswold limestone is a high-quality freestone that for centuries has been used for ashlar facings and other precision masonry. It was used in the construction or repair of Windsor Castle, St Paul's Cathedral, Blenheim Palace and most of the Oxford colleges. Sir Christopher Wren hired his master mason from Taynton to work on his churches and St Paul's in London.

Taynton thatch

Unlike the quarries at Windrush and Barrington, which were driven underground into the ridge that now carries the A40, the Taynton quarries were open. Now much overgrown, they are situated on private land a mile or so north of the village.

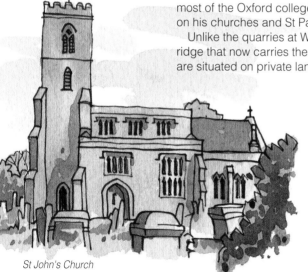

St John's Church

An avenue of yew trees line the broad path to the north door of St John the Evangelist's parish church. The slender tower houses a ring of six bells, two of them cast in Gloucester in 1717. Given Taynton's illustrious masonry history, it's not surprising that its handsome church features some wonderful examples of stonework, particularly the 15th-century font and carved corbel heads in the nave and north transept. A simple alms chest stands against the south wall, carved with the date 1609. The wooden roof is decorated with gilded rosettes and a central coiled serpent figure. There's also a fine collection of 18th-century table tombs in the churchyard.

Taynton has no visitor facilities.

Burford

This small medieval town built its reputation on wool, quarrying and coaching but nowadays it's regarded as the southern gateway to the Cotswolds and a huge magnet for tourists.

Burford's wealth was based on sheep, the long heavy fleeces of the famed Cotswold 'Lions', producing some of the best wool in Europe. Stone from the area was used to build some of England's finest buildings and Burford itself.

It was also an important staging post on the main Oxford to Gloucester route, with some 40 horse-drawn coaches a day passing through. Numerous hotels, inns and alehouses were build to support the trade. Unsurprisingly, brewing became an important local industry. 'Beware the Burford Bait' was a warning not to overeat the town's many hostelries. With the number of tempting teashops in today's town the lure of 'Burford Bait' is still thriving.

In coaching days the 15th-century bridge at the bottom of High Street carried most of the traffic between the Midlands and the south coast. Unfortunately it still does, but the stout stone bridge has so far resisted the pressures of highway improvers and motorists still have to queue at traffic lights to cross.

TOUR 5
From Tayton

St John the Baptist Church

Cob Hall

Almshouses

P Free

RIVER WINDRUSH

PRIORY LN

A361

HIGH ST

CHURCH LANE

SHEEP ST

WITNEY ST

POTTS LN

The Great House

THE HILL

SWAN LANE

Tolsey Museum

BARNS LANE

A40

A40

TOUR 6
To Shilton

The bad news for motorists coming from the north is that you'll probably have to face a long queue to get into the town. The good news is that once you're over the bridge all parking in Burford is free, though there are time restrictions on parts of High Street.

The medieval bridge over the Windrush

75

Burford's broad High Street slopes gracefully down from the wolds to the willow-fringed River Windrush and an inviting view of open countryside beyond. No two buildings in the street are the same. A roof line of higgledy-piggledy delight displays a medley of features that you'll see all over the Cotswolds – lopsided mullioned windows, dinky dormers, half-timbered façades with bow-legged beams, grand stone houses and yards with broad archways for horse and carriage access. A miscellany of shops, restaurants, tearooms, hotels and inns as varied as the architecture make Burford an excellent location for a rewarding urban stroll.

High Street

The oldest part of the town lies between the bridge and Sheep Street. Cob Hall, so called because it was once the Swan Inn (a cob is an adult male swan), was first recorded in 1590.

Across the road is the rather severe-looking Burford school which has been educating day and boarder pupils since 1571.

Cob Hall

Houses in Sheep Street

Tolls were once paid at the Tolsey, a 16th-century room built on stone pillars at the corner of High Street and Sheep Street. Once the medieval market building, a clock is still held out to the street as if time was important in this timeless setting. It now houses a small museum exhibiting Burford's social, cultural and industrial past. Until the early 20th century the town fire engine was kept below it.

There are some lovely houses in Sheep Street with an old brewery building next door to the 15th-century Lamb Inn. Further along the street stands the 17th-century Bay Tree Hotel, once the home of Sir Lawrence Tanfield, James I's Chancellor of the Exchequer, whose elaborate mausoleum is a striking feature in the church.

The Tolsey

The former George Hotel

The former George Hotel in High Street, opposite the junction with Witney Street, is reputed to have been where Charles II once stayed with Nell Gwyn during Bibury race week. Burford had its own race course at Aldsworth, three miles to the south, which held regular meetings for over 200 years before ending in 1802. The George was once Burford's leading coaching inns, dating back to the 14th century and boasts some graffiti etched onto an old windowpane by Samuel Pepys. Its distinctive archway survives and the building now houses an upmarket antiques shop.

The almshouses on Church Green, just outside the churchyard, were founded by Warwick the King-Maker in 1457, when he was Lord of the Manor of Burford, and partly rebuilt in 1828. Further along Church Lane, the Great House is just that, large and impressive. The 17th-century Palladian mansion is thought to have been built by master-mason Christopher Kempster, whose monument in the church includes a weeping cherub, carved by his son. The house doesn't appear to perform any modern function – except looking great. You can follow a tranquil footpath along the riverside from the car park.

St John the Baptist's Church dates back to the 12th century with its tower heightened and the tall spire added in the 14th century when Burford's prosperity from the wool trade was at its height. The magnificent south porch has an elegant tracery-panelled façade.

Unusually, the church's many mausoleums and chapels escaped the ravages of the 16th-century Reformation. Henry VIII's barber and surgeon, Edmund Harman has a funerary plaque in the nave which depicts four Amazonian figures, thought to be the earliest representation of Native Americans in Britain, even though it's unlikely that Harman every met any.

The font bears a crudely carved inscription, *Anthony Sedley Prisner 1649,* one of the 'Levellers', members of Oliver Cromwell's New Model Army who mutinied after they had to fight without pay. While in the town, 340 of them were seized by Cromwell's cavalry and locked in the church. Two days later three supposed ringleaders were taken into the churchyard and shot while their comrades were forced to watch from the church roof. A plaque near the church entrance pays tribute to their sacrifice and the Levellers have been heroes to left-wing politicians ever since.

The wealth of wool traders who once lived in the area is reflected in the number of extravagant 'bale tombs' in the churchyard. Unique to the Cotswolds, their rounded tops are reminiscent of a bale of wool.

Food & Drink

Burford hospitality has been famous for centuries and modern gastroculture is now well represented in the town. Stick to the familiar chains or try something more local or unusual. **Huffkins** in High Street was established in 1890 and is now a legendary craft bakery, tearoom and coffee shop. **Lynwood & Co** in the same street brings the down-to-earth and family-oriented coffee culture of Sydney to the Cotswolds with great coffee and granola, home-made cakes, sandwiches and salads. Traditionalists love the **Lamb Inn** in Sheep Street, a charming olde world inn with award winning food, restful ambiance and traditional Sunday lunches. For something different try the **Spice Lounge** in High Street, a highly-rated upmarket Indian restaurant and take-away with the emphasis on organic and creative dishes. Housed in a 15th-century former coaching inn, **The Bull** in High Street serves modern European influenced food in a rustic-chic bistro restaurant with a welcoming bar and outdoor seating.

St John the Baptist Church

Burford to Bibury · 22 miles

Burford – Shilton – Kencot – Filkins – Eastleach – Southrop – Fairford – Quenington – Hatherop – Coln St Aldwyns – Bibury

From Burford we head south with Brize Norton airfield in earshot to the lovely village of Shilton. After a call at tiny Kencot we visit industrious Filkins. A narrow lane then takes us across open high country to Eastleach, a Cotswold classic. Turning south, we follow the course of the River Leach to Southrop and the luxury 'village in a village' of Tyme, its tiny church the venue for a super-model's wedding. Crossing farmland brings us Fairford where the magnificent church houses a unique collection of late-medieval stained glass. Cotswold Water Park is nearby. The route now follows the valley of the River Coln to historic Quenington, then climbs to Hatherop and on to Coln St Aldwyns, edged by the lush water meadows of the Coln. Our tour ends along the ancient Salt Way, crossing open countryside with vast views to the tourist honey pot of Bibury.

ATTRACTIONS

1 Cotswold Woollen Weavers, Filkins

VILLAGE INNS

2 Rose & Crown, Shilton
3 Five Alls, Filkins
4 Victoria Inn, Eastleach
5 Swan, Southrop
6 Keepers Arms, Quenington
7 New Inn, Coln St Andrews

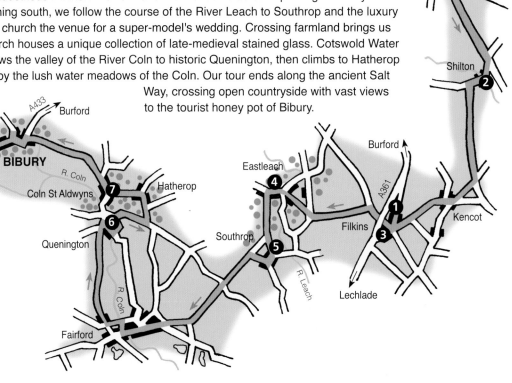

The Tour

Head east (signed Witney) from the A40 roundabout at the southern end of Burford for a short distance, then turn right onto the B4020, signed Faringdon. After around 1¾ miles turn right onto an unclassified road signed Shilton.

The Rose & Crown

Shilton

Away from busy roads, Shilton lies in the shelter of the valley of the Shill Brook, a tributary of the Thames, which flows languidly through the village from its source in the hamlet of Signet, a couple of miles upstream. Carterton, the sprawling 'garrison town' of the RAF base at Brize Norton is close by, but despite the whine of jet engines, Shilton is a village of picture-postcard perfection. It has all the attributes – a stream with a ford, a pond with a lively gaggle of ducks, cared-for cottages with colourful gardens, an ancient church and a friendly old inn. The ford was a location for the BBC's flagship series, *Downton Abbey*.

❷ Rose & Crown

Traditional 17th-century Cotswold stone inn with original beams, log fires and a large garden. Freehold and run by the owner, it's a popular 'local' and a destination food pub with a number of awards.

Open: Mon-Fri 11.30am-3pm & 6-10pm
Sat: 11-30am-10pm Sun: noon-9pm
Tel: 01993 842280
www.roseandcrownshilton.com

Church Lane curves up the hill from the ford to the beautifully humble and unadorned Church of the Holy Rood, which dates to around 1150 with many Norman features. Vestiges of colourful wall painting adorn the nave arches. Don't miss the square font, exquisitely carved with scenes from the crucifixion. Rood is an Old English word for a crucifix.

The ford across Shill Brook

Church of the Holy Rood

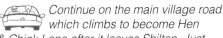

Continue on the main village road which climbs to become Hen & Chick Lane after it leaves Shilton. Just beyond the village turn left, signed Kencot 2½. At a fork in the road go right onto the A4477, signed Kencot. Turn right again at the next T-junction into the village. Go right opposite the Old Rectory on an unsigned road to the village centre.

Kencot

Village green & St George's Church

Another pretty village in earshot of the Brize Norton jets, Kencot has a delightful green too good to miss. St George's Church by the green is of late 12th-century origin and features a tower with a curious side turret giving it an unfortunate unfinished look. The Norman south doorway has a carved relief of Sagittarius slaying a monster. One door pillar has two Crusader Crosses. Knights carved one cross on their departure to the Crusades and another on their safe return. The font is 12th century with a 17th-century wooden cover and the pulpit Jacobean. The church interior was restored in 1962, made possible a notice reveals, *'by the generosity of Edith Bundy of San Francisco'.*

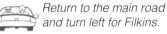

Return to the main road and turn left for Filkins.

Filkins

Cotswold Woollen Weavers

Shop & Post Office

TOUR

From Kencot **TOUR**

The Five Alls

A361

BROADWELL BROOK

A4477

Swinford Museum

St John's, Filkins

St John's, Broughton Poggs

Separated by a riverlet of water known as the Broadwell Brook, Filkins and Broughton Poggs are essentially one village. Now happily bypassed by the busy A361, Filkins is totally Cotswold in character and built from the stone on which it stands.

Stone is it's outstanding feature. Large slabs, known as planks, fastened together with iron clamps edge many of the cottage gardens, looking like impoverished headstones.

A local stonemason, George Swinford and village benefactor Sir John Cripps, established the Swinford Museum in the 1920s. It houses a fine collection of domestic, agricultural, trade and craft tools, but sadly is now open only infrequently.

Swinford Museum

St John's Church, Filkins

St John's Church in Filkins was built to a French Gothic style during 1855-7, designed by architect George Edmund Street, best known for his work on the Law Courts in London. Leading members of the Arts & Craft Movement, Clayton and Webb, manufactured the stained glass in the east window and William Morris was involved in the building's design.

St John's Church, Broughton Poggs

Different in both style and age, but also dedicated to St John, the church in Broughton Poggs is a small Norman building tucked away behind farm buildings opposite the wonderfully-named Dancing Trousers Cookery School. The small church has a squat saddleback tower and Norman features including small doorways, a narrow chancel arch and a tub-shaped font.

Filkins fizzes with community spirit and boasts a village hall, shop and post office plus, even more unusual in the Cotswolds, an outdoor swimming pool which can be enjoyed by all villagers and families from the surrounding area.

The Five Alls

❸ The Five Alls

An 18th-century coaching house which combines rustic atmosphere with London restaurant service. A flag stone bar and a comfy lounge with sofas by the fire is the setting for award winning food with a Mediterranean influence. A dedicated local clientele and a sprinkling of famous personalities complete the feel-good vibe. There's also nine rooms to let including a family room

Open for food: Mon-Thu noon-2.30pm & 6-9.30pm Fri-Sun noon-3pm & 6-10pm (closed for dinner on Sundays)
Bar: Mon-Sat noon-11pm Sun noon-9pm
Tel: 01367 860875
www.thefiveallsfilkins.co.uk

❶ Cotswold Woollen Weavers

Housed in a beautiful 18th-century barn designing and making fine woollen cloth since 1982 on traditional machines. Upmarket fashion collections of clothing, rugs and home accessories. Licensed coffeeshop and restaurant with art exhibition and picnic blankets (woollen of course) for warm afternoons in the orchard.

Open every day from New Year to Christmas Eve. Mon-Sat 10am-6pm
Sun 2-6pm
Tel:01367 860660
www.cotswoldwoollenweavers.co.uk

Leave Filkins on the road behind St Peter's church, signed Barringtons 6. Beyond the village go under the A361 and turn left signed Barringtons. After a short distance take the first left onto a narrow unclassified road signed Eastleach. Keep on the road through open country for around 2 miles before dropping downhill into Eastleach.

Eastleach

As you turn into the village a vision of extreme loveliness is gradually revealed. Even by Cotswold standards, Eastleach is something special. Sir John Betjeman, the poet and doyen of 'Englishness', declared it to be his favourite Cotswold village and few visitors would disagree.

This is actually two settlements, Eastleach Turville and Eastleach Martin, each with its own parish church, a few minutes walk apart, on either side of the River Leach. Turville is the largest these days, but Martin has the bigger church.

Founded by one of William the Conquer's knights, Richard Fitz Pons, and dedicated to St Michael and St Martin, the present church is mostly 13th century. A few Norman features survive including some interesting decorated Gothic windows terminating in tiny carved heads, but the interior is relatively plain. No longer used for worship since 1981, the building is maintained by the Churches Preservation Trust.

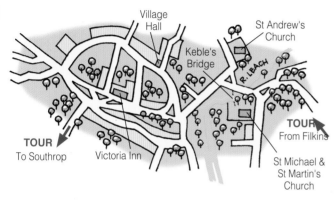

Village Hall

St Andrew's Church

Keble's Bridge

R. LEACH

TOUR
From Filkins

TOUR
To Southrop

Victoria Inn

St Michael & St Martin's Church

Church of St Michael & St Martin

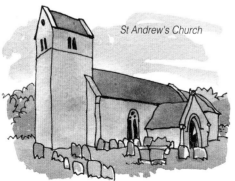
St Andrew's Church

St Andrew's is generally considered to be the most interesting of the two churches with an early 14th-century Norman tower and a simple saddleback roof. Its most prominent feature is the *Christ in Majesty* tympanum over the west door. Inside there's a fine canopied tomb and a pleasing pulpit with a lectern said to have come from the abbey at Tewkesbury.

In 1867 St Thomas Bazley of Hatherop became Lord of the Manor and built many of the later buildings in Turville including the almshouse in the main street, the clock tower and adjoining buildings, plus several cottages.

Keble's clapper bridge

Victoria Inn

❹ Victoria Inn

A traditional, cosy, country pub once an early 18th-century private house with attached coach house. Turned into a pub in 1856 and acquired by Arkell's in 1976. Extensive menu using locally sourced ingredients, including venison, pheasant and pigeon. Big Sunday lunches.

Bar open every day: 11am-11pm
Food: Mon noon-2pm Tue-Sat noon-2pm
& 6.30-9pm Sun noon-3pm
Tel: 01367 850277
www.thevictoriaineastleach.co.uk

Take time to wander around Turville, crossing the stone road bridge over the river and climbing past the war memorial to enjoy the views – and the hospitality – at the Victoria Inn. Return down the hill to admire the colourful gardens and take the footpath to the lovely clapper bridge over the river into St Michael's churchyard. It was named Keble's Bridge after John Keble who was church curate during the early 19th century. In early spring the banks of the river are ablaze with daffodils, attracting many admirers – and their cameras.

The Turville clocktower and road to Southrop

Leave on the road opposite the inn, signed Southrop 1¼ & Fairford 4. The road may be narrow but the fields on both sides seem to go on forever, amazingly flat and fertile.

Southrop

Straddling the Gloustershire-Oxfordshire border, Southrop is set amongst the willows and water meadows of the River Leach, the last place of any consequence before it joins the Thames near Lechlade.

St Peter's Church

Accessed behind the buildings of Thyme Farm, the small and modest St Peter's Church lacks a tower but is regarded as the oldest and best preserved Norman church in the county. It also contains a remarkable 12th-century font, discovered built into the south doorway by John Keble, curate from 1823-5. This treasure, with symbolic carvings of the Virtues trampling on the Vices, attracts admirers from near and far. Model Kate Moss and guitarist Jamie Hince were married at the church in 2011, attracting a slightly different class of admirers.

The 150-acre Southrop Manor Estate lies across the road from the Swan, mostly hidden by high stone walls. After a 12-year restoration of barns, cottages and houses it was opened as a luxury destination 'village within a village' and rebranded as 'Thyme'. More accessible cottages for ordinary visitors to appreciate are strung along the twisting Lechlade Road.

Swan Inn

 Swan Inn

An ivy-swathed 17th-century village pub expensively updated to a landmark country restaurant serving hearty, simple fare. Now part of the local Thyme luxury complex, there's still a bar for locals and a upmarket restaurant for the London fashion set.

Bar open Mon-Sun 11.30am-11pm
Restaurant: Lunch Mon-Fri noon-2.30pm
Sat & Sun noon-3pm
Dinner: Mon-Thu & Sun 6-9.30pm
Fri & Sat 6-10pm
Tel: 01367 8501741
www.thyme.co.uk

 Leave Southrop on Lechlade Road but ignore the road going left in the village signed Lechlade. About 400 yards further on swing left, signed Fairford 3. Join the A417 on the outskirts of Fairford and turn right to enter the town.

Market Place

Fairford

Once an important staging post on the London to Gloucester coaching run, the small market town of Fairford is bordered on two sides by the River Coln. Nearby are RAF Fairford, which holds a famous annual tattoo, and the Cotswold Water Park; pits from 60 years of gravel attraction transformed into more than 100 lakes for a host of leisure activities

The busy A417 slices through the town and attractive, ancient, silver-stoned cottages – some half-timbered – line the narrow entry from the east, but it's around the broad Market Place where most interest is centred. The charming Bull Hotel dominates the square with an attractive half-timbered building on the corner, once the George Inn.

A magnificent example of Perpendicular Gothic architecture, St Mary's Church stands proudly at the top of High Street. The rich sculptural details on Its massive central tower include the arms of John Tame, one of the Cotswold's greatest – and richest – wool merchants. His son Edmund built the church in the 1490s and it has attracted visitors ever since. The magnet is the only complete set of medieval stained glass windows in the British Isles. Know as 'the poor man's bible' they tell the pictorial story of the Catholic faith in glowing jewel-like colours and are attributed to Barnard Flower, Master Glass Painter to Henry VII.

Among the table tombs and several servicemen's graves in the churchyard there's a poignant stone memorial to Tiddles, the church cat who fell off the church roof.

St Mary's Church

Continue on the A417 through Fairford, crossing the Coln on a tight bend. At a small green just before the Marlborough Arms, turn right into Coronation Street signed Quenington 2 & Coln St Aldwyns 2½.

North doorway of St Swithin's Church

On the outskirts of Quenington turn right at a large green, signed Quenington Village. Pass the Keepers Arms on your left. You may be able to park near the church, otherwise with consideration at the roadside.

The first of the three villages we'll visit along the valley of the Coln as it twists its way downstream from Bibury. Quenington is a large village with striking Cotswold stone cottages widely spread across slopes above the river. Opposite a large green on the outskirts we pass the village hall, which was used as a chapel from 1926 until 2010, becoming the hall in 2013.

Quenington

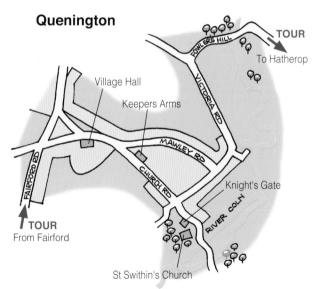

FOWLERS HILL

VICTORIA RD

TOUR
To Hatherop

Village Hall

Keepers Arms

MAWLEY RD

CHURCH RD

FAIRFORD RD

Knight's Gate

RIVER COLN

TOUR
From Fairford

St Swithin's Church

Built during the late 11th-century, the church of St Swithin was first dedicated to the Virgin Mary. It was then rededicated to St Swithin following the 16th-century Reformation. Grade 1 listed, the highest category, the building is notable for the wonderful Norman carvings above the two 12th-century doors.

The north door shows a traditional Norman chevron pattern incised on three levels. This surrounds an earlier tympanum depicting the *Harrowing of Hell* or the *Descent of Jesus into Hell* to defeat evil and release the souls trapped there. This was a common theme in medieval mystery plays and occurs frequently in Norman relief carvings.

Above the south doorway, the *Coronation of the Virgin*, said to be the oldest representation in Europe still in situ, is possibly a reference to the church's earlier dedication.

Unfortunately, the interior of the church cannot match the glories of its doors. It was extensively restored in the 1880s by the architect who restored Gloucester Cathedral, Frederick Waller, but with a result here that's best described as 'well-intentioned'.

Keepers Arms

❻ Keepers Arms

A family-run country pub serving home cooked food using fresh locally sourced ingredients with great ale at sensible prices. Children and dogs welcome. There are four characterful Cotswold style bedrooms to let. The pub has been included in the Camra Good Beer Guide since 2011 and won Channel 4's programme *'Four in a Bed'* in 2015.

**Bar open: Mon-Tue 6-10.30pm,
Wed-Sat noon-3pm & 6-11pm
Sun noon-4pm & 7-10.30pm
Food served: Wed-Sat noon-2pm &
6-9pm Sun noon-3.30pm
Kitchen closed Sun evening & all day
Mon and Tue
Tel: 01285 750349
www.thekeepersarms.co.uk**

Quenington Court, a mainly 19th-century house near the church, stands on the site of a preceptory of the Knight's Templar, which later passed into the hands of the Knight's Hospitaller. The gatehouse, known as Knight's Gate, survives, Grade 1 listed. Thought to date from the 14th century, it was partly rebuilt and extended in the early 16th century.

Nearby there's a remarkable stone-built dovecot, of similar vintage, with a conical slate roof topped by a lantern lid providing access for the doves to 600 nesting boxes inside. The preceptory also had two mills on the river, one now a desirable private house.

Historical records also mention a moat, which though no longer existing, might be the foundation of several fish ponds west of the gatehouse.

Knight's Gate

The dovecote

 Head up Victoria Road to leave Quenington and climb across the hillside above the river to a T-junction. Turn right signed Hetherop 4 and Lechlade 5½.

🚗 *Climb past some fine Cotswold stone houses with magnificent views. After about a mile you reach a flat hilltop. Take the hairpin junction left, signed Hatherop ¼ and Bibury 4. At the village school in Hatherop turn left signed Coln St Andrews 1 and Bibury 3¼. Pass Hatherop Castle School where there's an interesting church, before entering Coln St Aldwyn's.*

Hatherop

Church of St Nicholas

The parish church of St Nicholas stands beside the manor house, now Hatherop Castle School. The medieval church was rebuilt by Lord de Mauley in 1854 in French Gothic style, and features an ornate mortuary chapel by William Burgess. Within the chapel is a marble memorial to Lady de Mauley (died 1844) by Raffaelle Monti.

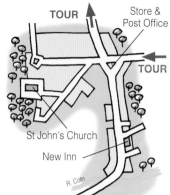

Coln Store and Post Office was originally a 16th-century poor house owned by the church. In the early 19th century it was used as a school for girls in the village. A bakery situated in an adjacent outbuilding is still used today, baking bread and pasties for sale in the store.

The small café serves freshly brewed tea and coffee with sandwiches, salads and hot snacks. There's also a pleasant seating area in the garden.

Coln St Aldwyns

A traditional estate village made up of cottages and houses of pale Cotswold stone. The main street starts in the water meadows of the Coln – where a house displays a mill wheel to acknowledge its industrial heritage – then climbs up the hill to a tiny raised green shaded by a magnificent horse chestnut tree. Nearby a telephone is housed in a beautiful stone box with a pyramid-shaped roof of slate – Cotswold, of course.

Village Store & Post Office

The Church of St John the Baptist dates from the 13th century, with the tower added in the 15th century. There's impressive Norman chevron work and fearsome dragon's heads on the south doorway. Overhead, a man is chased by a demon while a cat-like creature looks on. The door itself is centuries old. Sadly, after this dramatic entry, the church interior is disappointing, the result of a radical restoration in the 1850's.

The Elizabethan manor house next door to the churchyard overlooks the Coln and was built by a Quaker family who used it for meetings where it became a hot-bed of political Non-Conformity. Later, Hatherop Castle School bought it and used the manor as a sixth-form annex from 1967-1974. It was eventually sold to a developer and converted into six residential units.

 New Inn

A highly-regarded gastronome destination with 14 letting rooms. Currently undergoing a change of management with reopening scheduled for March 2019.

Phone 01285 750651
www.thenewinncoln.co.uk

St John the Baptist Church

New Inn

 To continue to Bibury turn right at the post office signed Bibury 2½, and beyond the village turn left, opposite the entrance to The Old Dairy onto an unclassified road, Salt Way, signed Bibury. Cross flat farmland with extensive views before joining the B4425, turning left to go down the hill into Bibury and the end of this tour.

Arlington Row

Bibury

One of England's oldest working trout farms, the Bibury Trout Farm was founded in 1902 by the famous naturalist Arthur Severn to stock local rivers and streams with native Brown Trout.

The hatchery now spawns up to six million trout ova every year. The only fee-paying attraction in the village, it's always busy. You can catch fish from a network of ponds and buy fresh and smoked trout to barbecue (strictly only on the farm's barbies) in several picnic areas. There's also a café where tempting trout dishes are included on the menu.

Set in a shallow, steep-sided valley of the River Coln, the small village of Bibury tries to live up to Victorian designer William Morris' excessive description as 'surely the most beautiful in Britain' with modest success.

Parking is extremely difficult in the village and totally inadequate for the cavalcade of tour coaches and thousands of motorists who visit. There's a small car park opposite the trout farm and roadside parking alongside the river. You might also be lucky finding somewhere to park in the one-way street past the church.

Arlington Row, a row of nine Cotswold cottages, has graced many a card and calendar and was so admired by Henry Ford he wanted to export them to America. Thankfully, they were saved for restoration in 1930.

Originally built around 1380 as a wool store, the building was converted in the 17th century to house weavers. 'National Treasure' status was endowed on the scene after it was printed inside British passports.

Arlington Mill

Believed to date back to the 17th Century, Arlington Mill once fulled (cleaned) the cloth produced in Arlington Row. After a period housing an excellent museum of local industrial life, the mill is now a private residence.

St Mary's Church

St Mary's Church is blessedly located in a quieter (and more attractive) part of the village. Surrounded by fine houses, the Church of St Mary, Anglo-Saxon in origins, is a handsome local stone building with a fine collection of table tombs in the churchyard.

The inside doesn't disappoint either with much to see, including Saxon and Norman carvings, medieval windows, stained glass and a striking chancel arch with evidence of Saxon, Norman, and Early English work. The stained glass window in the north chancel wall, designed in 1927 by Karl Parsons, featured on the 1992 Christmas stamps set issued by the Royal Mail.

Swan Hotel and road bridge

Nobody visits Bibury for the shopping (unless it's for trout) but most everyday items are available in the village.

The trout farm shop sells fresh bread, milk, butter and cheese, along with newspapers and magazines.

Nestled alongside the river, the pretty little post office sells groceries, hot sausage rolls and pasties, and also stocks a unique collection of souvenirs and gifts.

17th-century footbridge over the Coln

Food & Drink

Sadly, there's not a lot of choice. However, Bibury's only pub, the **Catherine Wheel**, is a good bet with a modest gastro menu. It's off the tourist mainstream and predictably busy. You'll find it up the road past Arlington Mill. The ivy-clad **Swan Hotel** looks welcoming enough in its picturesque setting, but the ambiance is more that of an upmarket hotel than a drop-in restaurant. Set in a Jacobean mansion overlooking the church, **Bibury Court** is a tranquil hotel with an excellent restaurant. Popular for posh afternoon tea – with prices to match.

Unfortunately, the modern concept of ubiquitous coffee shops seems to have passed Bibury by.

The Coln runs shallow through the village and is so full of fish and water weed there's barely room for all the ducks and moorhens. It's crossed by attractive footbridges and a 1770 road bridge.

Bibury has a lot of charm and William Morris wasn't all wrong. But considering some of the gorgeous villages we've visited on this tour, he wasn't all right either.

Bibury to Northleach · 22 miles

Bibury – Ablington – Winson – Coln Rogers – Coln St Dennis – Fossebridge – Chedworth – Yanworth – Withington – Compton Abgate – Hampnett – Northleach

The A429 Fosse Way is the only north-south artery through the Cotswolds and on this section both sides of the road are sparsely populated with quiet villages and ancient churches tucked into the hills. Ablington is pleasant enough but there's little to delay us here. Trim, tidy and rural, Winson, Coln Rogers and Coln St Denis are set along the Coln river. At the A429, the Inn at Fossebridge dominates a dip in the road. The farm shop on the outskirts of Chedworth is worth stopping for before the picturesque entry into the village around the Seven Tuns Inn. The route now climbs up the increasingly remote Coln Valley to the estate village of Yanworth with its weathered Norman church and incredible views. We descend to the wondrous Roman Villa on the other side of the valley, said to be some 1,500 years old and in remarkable condition. In contrast, Withington seems positively modern, with a railway (closed 1961) and an old inn (built 1960), but the magnificent church is comfortably aged, dating to the 15th century. We now climb steeply through an attractively lonely landscape to Compton Abgate, before rejoining the 21st century on the busy A40. A turn off into a narrow lane takes us through Hampnett, a classic Cotswold mix of lazy streams, cottages in rolling fields and barn conversions. Northleach is only a mile or so away and the end of this varied tour.

ATTRACTIONS
❶ Chedworth Farm Shop
❷ Roman Villa, Chedworth

CAFÉS
❸ Chedworth Farm Shop
❹ Roman Villa, Chedworth

VILLAGE INNS
❺ Inn at Fossebridge
❻ Seven Tuns, Chedworth
❼ Mill Inn, Withington

The Tour

*Leave Bibury on the road past the Swan Hotel
signed Ablington ¾ & Northleach 5.*

Ablington

Ancient barns

The Coln valley, with its soft folds, open downs and riverside meadows are the essence of the central Cotswold landscape. Our journey upstream begins at the hamlet of Ablington, clinging to the hillside by the river.

As you enter the settlement between high stone walls, a large grey-stone mansion stands on your right, Ablington House, built around 1600. The stone lions on top of the gateposts once

graced the Houses of Parliament. It had a spell as an atmospheric B&B but is now a private residence.

Opposite the red phone box at the village centre look through the trees on your right for two ancient barns, part of Manor Farm. The larger one was built in the mid to late 16th century, probably just after the Dissolution of the Monasteries. It has a gabled wagon porch and a fine raised-cruck roof. The smaller barn,

Ablington House

built up against it has a similar roof. It carries a datestone 'IC/1727 - John Coxwell'. John Coxwell was the lord of the manor at that time. The barns are still in agricultural use, being fitted out as stables.

On your left a high stone wall hides most of Ablington Manor, which dominates the village. It's one of those ancient, hidden-away places that, after the dissolution of the monasteries, gained status in the time of the Tudors as the seat of a prosperous trader.

John Coxwell made his money in the burgeoning wool trade and built the present house in about 1590. It underwent various alterations in succeeding centuries, but the appealing, multi-gabled house sits in a place of great natural beauty, seemingly little altered by the passing of time. It was once the home of Arthur Gibbs, the young squire who immortalised Ablington in *A Cotswold Village*, the first of the classics to look at late 16th-century country life with poetic insight.

Further along the road you come to a minute green where the road swings left to cross the Coln. Pause on the bridge for a moment for a lovely view of the river and the stone bridge entrance to the Manor.

Climb from Ablington and turn right at a tee junction signed Winson 1 and Fossebridge 3. Cross rolling countryside with occasional glimpses of the River Coln through trees on your right. At a large roadside barn on the outskirts of Winson turn right, signed Village only.

Winson

The minute village of Winson sits in the hollow of a Cotswold hill, bounded to the east by the River Coln. Despite having no shop, post office or pub and a population of around ninety, fewer than half of them full-time residents, the settlement is full of interest and worth having a stroll around. You can park with discretion at the triangular green in front of the manor house.

The small Church of St Michael sits poised on the highest point of the

St Michael's Church

village above a fine group of farm buildings. It has a typical Cotswold-style bellcote, a Norman south doorway and a chancel with quaint Victorian wall paintings. There are 18th-century table tombs in the neat churchyard and some fine views across the village.

The elegant manor house overlooking the green dates from 1740, built for Richard Howse, Surgeon-General to the Army. A well-proportioned, though small, classical house in which the eminent Scottish architect, James Gibbs, (who designed St. Martin-in-the-Fields in London) is thought to have had a planning input.

Take a walk along Ditch Lane past the red phone box where a line of classic Cotswold houses with colourful gardens leads to a delightful fairy-tale thatched cottage on the hillside.

Despite the influx of multi-millionaires

The manor house

turning agricultural workers' cottages into luxury weekend retreats, Winson remains a haven of peace, a world away from the tourist hot-spot of Bibury, just a few miles away down river.

Winson thatch

At the northern end of Winson turn right signed Fossebridge 2¼ and Coln Rogers ¾. At Winson Mill Farm go left signed Coln Rogers ½ and Coln St Dennis 1¼. Cross the Coln on the outskirts of Coln St Rogers and bear right signed Coln St Rogers 1 and Fossebridge 1¾.

Coln Rogers

A tranquil Cotswold hamlet, named after a 12th-century knight, Roger de Gloucester, Coln Rogers lies on level ground where the river has broadened and woods clothe its banks. The main single street is pretty enough but the village's main feature is its Saxon church.

Coln Rogers' main street

Tucked away down a lane from the road, the parish church of St Andrew is a hidden gem that preserves many of the original 11th-century Saxon features including parts of the nave and chancel. The frame for one of the windows in the north wall of the chancel is made from a single piece of stone. The simple stone pulpit dates from the 15th century. A beautiful plaque inside the porch of the church commemorates the fact that Coln Rogers is a 'thankful village' as all the men from the district who fought in the First World War returned safely.

St Andrew's Church

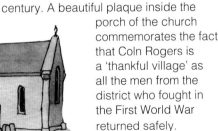

Lane to the church

Climb beyond Coln Rogers through open countryside. Swing right at Pindrup, a large 17th-century farmhouse into Coln St Dennis.

Coln St Dennis

The most northern of the three Coln villages, picturesque Coln St Dennis climbs up a gentle hill from the river's water meadows. A small green marks the village centre with the church on your right and a beautiful 17th-century grey-stone house by the roadside on your left. The village takes its name from its ownership in the Middle Ages, when it belonged to the abbey of St. Denis, Paris, gifted to it by William the Conqueror.

Keep straight on past the church and turn left at a large barn into a narrow lane that takes you through a delightful cluster of honey-coloured Cotswold cottages. At a T-junction turn right and continue climbing. The manor house stands just to your left below the junction.

Dating to the 17th century, the manor house was built of rubble with stone mullioned windows and quoins, moulded and fluted chimney-stacks, and a Cotswold stone roof. Extended in 1861, it was also substantially altered and extended in 1965.

The house is thought to have been originally built by the Mortimer family, the only lords of the manor before the 20th century to live in the parish. In 1672 it was occupied by Charles Turk and was reported to have had 'six hearths'. The lords of the manor liked to keep warm.

St James's Church

Manor house

The parish church of Saint James the Great sits in a tranquil spot by the river away from the main village. Apart from the top of the squat tower the church is almost entirely Norman, with the addition of some Decorated Gothic and Perpendicular Gothic windows, and several interesting 17th-century wall monuments.

The Normans rarely built central towers on their churches and the one on St James's is supported by massive buttresses. When the belfry was added to the tower in the 15th century the extra weight caused part of the eastern arch to collapse.

The magnificent wooden door on the 16th-century porch has the date 1637 intriguingly carved into it with the initials THH. Perhaps the builder who installed the door?

Look out for the weird collection of Norman corbel figures supporting the nave roof. An ancient clock was replaced in 1957 by an electric one, donated by members of the Price family, descendants of an earlier rector.

Leave Coln St Dennis, turning sharp left at a farmyard and continue to the A429 at Fossebridge. Turn left signed Roman Villa 3½ to The Inn at Fossebury. Continue on the A429 for about ¾ of a mile beyond the inn, then turn right at a tee junction signed Chedworth and Withington. Bear left at Chedworth Farm Shop and after a mile or so through pleasant farmland turn right, signed Yanworth 3½, into Chedworth Village.

The hamlet of Fossebridge developed in the 18th century, probably due to the increase in traffic along the Fosse Way after it was turnpiked in 1755. Around a dozen stone houses now make up a narrow street leading off the main road. The dip in the A429 is dominated by the large creeper-covered inn.

Chedworth farm Shop is situated a mile or so before Chedworth village but no matter, it's still a good place to stop – especially if you're an ice cream aficionado.

Fossebridge

Inn at Fossebridge

Chedworth Farm Shop

⑤ Inn at Fossebury

Billed 'The Cotswolds Favourite County Inn', this 18th-century former coaching inn is prominently situated on a dip on the Roman Fosse Way. The attractive bar boasts old timbers, a fine flagstone floor and open fires. With nine traditionally-styled rooms to let, there's also four acres of garden with the River Coln flowing through, and a lake. Children, walkers and dogs welcome.

Bar open daily from noon for lunch & dinner
Tel: 01285 720721
www.fossebridgeinn.co.uk

❶ Chedworth Farm Shop

A cheery family-run part of Denfurlong farm with 'home-grown' products, including fresh veg and free-range eggs, sold in the shop They also serve big breakfasts, light lunches and afternoon treats in the café or outside in a 'village green' area. The fabulous home-made ice cream, made from the milk of cows on the farm, is worth stopping for on its own. Also served as milkshake in a traditional tall glass.

Open: Mon-Thu & Sat 9am-5pm Fri 9am-4pm Sun & Bank holidays 9am-4pm

Coming from the farm shop you arrive at a large green where you turn right, signed Yanworth 3½, into the village of Chedworth. Continue across a terrace overlooking the lower village and turn left at a 'Y-junction, signed Yanworth 2¼ & Withington 3. Pass a red phone box and descend into a wooded area with a small triangular green where you can probably park. The Seven Tuns Inn is nearby, down the narrow village road signed Stowell 2¼ & Yanworth 2¼.

Chedworth

Set amid a patchwork of fields on steep hillsides bounding the River Coln, Chedworth is a large village spread linearly along a quiet valley. The railway branch line between Cheltenham and Andover once ran through here but was closed in 1961. Remnants of the station, bridges and track can still be found in the lower part of the village

The best part of Chedworth is around the Seven Tuns Inn where a spring bubbles out of a wall across the road and a path climbs past a string of fine 18th-century cottages to the church. Steep-pitched gables and mullioned windows typify the Cotswold style in large and small houses alike.

Despite its apparent isolation, Chedworth is a thriving community with a village school, hall, church, pub, farm shop and campsite, plus a wide range of clubs and societies. A full colour parish magazine is published ten times a year and is can be to downloaded online.

❻ Seven Tuns Inn

Attractive 17th-century stone-built village pub, recently reopened as a free house. There are two bars and an old restored water wheel in the riverside garden. The pub is within walking distance of the Roman Villa and thus on the path of many walkers and ramblers. With an excellent range of home-made food and local ales, the inn was a recent winner of seasonal pub of the year for North Cotswold CAMRA. Parking for around 40 cars.

Open: Sun-Thu 11am-11pm
Fri & Sat 11am-12am
Food served: Mon-Fri noon-3pm &
6-9.30pm Sat noon-9.30pm Sun noon-
3.30pm & 6-9pm
Tel: 01285 720630
www.seventuns.co.uk

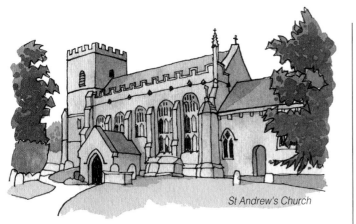

St Andrew's Church

St Andrew's Church has unusually large windows, installed in the 15th century when the nave had to be raised to accommodate them. The tower and a stout font, carved with interlaced arches, are 12th century, while the pulpit (hewn from a single block of stone), was a 15th-century addition.

Don't miss the copy of the 16th-century 'Breeches Bible', a Protestant translation, which describes Adam and Eve making 'breeches' out of fig leaves. As a contrast to all the old stuff, look out for the modern sculpture of the *Mother and Child* carved by Helen Rock in 1911.

 Leave Chedworth on the narrow village road (Queen Street) which climbs to open country. After about 1½ miles you arrive at a crossroads. Go straight across signed Stowell and Northleach. Climb through open farmland. At the next junction turn sharp left signed Yanworth ½. Turn right at the next T-junction into a narrow road signed Church and Church Farm, to Yanworth.

Yanworth

This is a remarkable example of a compact farming estate village with beautiful preserved farm buildings and mellow terraced cottages. Set on a hilltop,

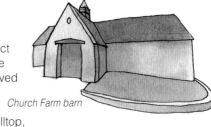

Church Farm barn

the view down the wooded Coln Valley is sensational. Like many remote settlements, tiny Yanworth has a strong sense of community with a village hall, a children's play area and a red phone box.

St Michael's Church stands in the yard of Church Farm, rather isolated from the rest of the village. It dates from the 12th and 15th centuries with a miniature tower standing flush with the west wall. Gargoyles can be seen on the north and south sides of the building but most have been defaced. Marks on the wall of the north transept are thought to be shrapnel damage from the English Civil War.

The church has a Norman south doorway with chevron mouldings, a Norman chancel arch and a stout font of around the same period. An odd wall-painting of Old Father Time (complete with scythe) is probably from a later period and could possibly refer to the church's location in a farmyard.

St Michael's Church

Keep on the village road, from the north end of Yanworth gradually descending for around 1½ miles into a densely wooded area. Soon after crossing the Coln you arrive at the junction with the lane to the Roman Villa. The car park is around 400 yards straight on. Turn right for Withington, signed 2½.

❷❹ Roman Villa

Discovered by a gamekeeper in 1864, this is one of the finest – and largest – Roman villa remains in Britain. Dating from 120-400AD, the beautifully preserved site includes more than fifty rooms, mosaic pavements, bath suites, heated living rooms and more. A Victorian hunting lodge plonked incongruously at its centre houses a museum of archaeological finds.

Admission fee. Café & shop. Seasonal opening times – check website. www.nationaltrust.org.uk/chedworth-roman-villa

Roman Villa

 The road continues through some 2½ miles of a spectacular mix of woods and open farmland following the course of the River Coln. Pass the Compton Gallery, a lonely but classy arts events venue, before descending into Withington. You arrive at a T-junction where turning left (unsigned) takes you to the main village and church (worth a detour despite all the double yellow lines at the roadsides) and turning right goes to Compton Abdale, the next part of the tour.

Withington

A large, pretty village split into two distinct parts by the River Coln and the now dismantled railway, Withington lies near the head of the river valley and from 1891 to 1961 had a railway station. Set on rising ground, the western side of the village is the most interesting with a picturesque High Street and an ancient and much admired church.

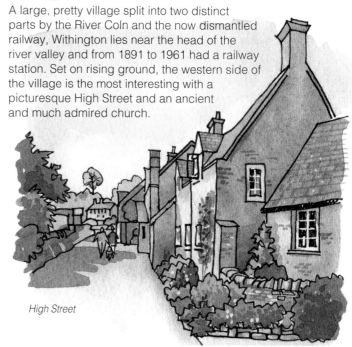

High Street

The imposing parish church of St Michael and All Angels dates from the 12th century but the site goes back even further to Saxon times when a monastery was established here in 674AD.

The building was altered in the 15th century when the Perpendicular clerestory and a taller tower were added, There are two splendid Norman doorways, both displaying exceptional decoration. An odd feature of the nave is that all the light comes from the clerestory windows, all the Norman window openings being blocked up.

St Michael & All Angels Church

The interior was ruthlessly purged by the Victorians but there are several interesting memorials including a wonderful over-the-top Jacobean one to Bridgett and John Howe and their eight children (looking suitably pious).

❼ Mill Inn

17th-century pub with a large beer garden beautifully situated by the River Coln. The building looks old but was actually rebuilt in 1960, but with weathered stone from Northleach Prison. There are several nice nooks and corners, beams, wood/flagstone floors, two inglenook log fires and a woodburner. Generous helpings of traditional pub food include basket meals in four dining rooms. The famous 'chicken in the basket' is claimed to have originated here. Children and dogs are welcome. Now owned by Samuel Smith Brewery and exclusively sells its beers.

Open: Mon-Wed noon-3pm & 5.30-10pm
Thu & Fri noon-11pm Sat 11.30am-11pm
Sun 11-30am-9pm
Tel: 01242 890204

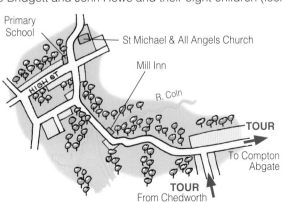

Mill Inn

🚗 *The road from Withington climbs through farmland for around 2 miles into Compton Abdale. Pass the church high on a hillside on your right and turn left signed Hazleton 1½ and Salperton 3.*

Compton Abdale

The village seen from the churchyard

This small, unassuming village snuggles down in a deep valley surrounded by steep rolling hills. There are few roads in this isolated part of Gloucestershire so its setting on a crossroads of narrow lanes, known as the Square, suggests that Compton Abdale may at one time have been a place of some importance. Though now a peaceful collection of classic Cotswold farms and homes, its the church – built into a steep bank overlooking the village – that's the main attraction.

St Oswald's dates back to the 13th century with a square Perpendicular tower capped by pinnacles at each corner. Each pinnacle bears a remarkable collection of monstrous heraldic beasts and grotesque gargoyles – but you may need binoculars to appreciate their fanciful detail.

The interior has suffered from 19th and 20th-century 'over-restorations' but a mutilated carving, said to be St George slaying the dragon, is worth a look.

Below the churchyard there's a stone 'crocodile' head at the roadside which spouts water from a powerful underground spring into a massive trough. It was the work of local mason, George Curtis, who died in 1887 aged 83. Apparently the carving was so ridiculed by the locals George took offence and left the village to end his days in Durham.

St Oswald's Church

When you reach the A40 from Compton Abdale turn right where a further ½ mile brings you to the Puesdown Inn. It dates from 1236 and was a highly regarded restaurant and hotel until being sold in 2018, since when it has been closed. The new owners plan to reopen the inn after renovation has been completed. Keep on the A40 and after around another 1½ miles take the turning on your right signed Hampnett Village only.

Lane from the upper village

Hampnett

The single track road brings you to the Saxon settlement of Hampnett, which consists of an intriguing trio of sub-villages with a large field at their centre near the source of the River Leach. The top part of the village is no more than a sparse collection of houses with a rough green where you can park.

The lane continues past the second part, set attractively down the hill on your right. The main village consists of a number of converted farm buildings clustered picturesquely around the church. St George's is mainly Norman and the muted colours of its exterior stone give no hint of the blaze of colour that awaits inside. The interior is decorated with amazing Victorian stencilling, painted in a floral design with angelic figures, the idea of the Rev Wiggins, vicar of Hampnett in 1868. The effect is startling and some of it, especially on the ribbed vaulting of the chancel, is quite beautiful.

The main village & St George's Church

Hampnett barn conversions

Continue on the single road alongside a wood know as Prison Copse and turn right at the junction with the A429 to the Old Prison, where the road opposite takes you into Northleach and the end of this tour.

The Old Prison entrance

Standing somberly at the side of the old Fosse Way on the outskirts of Northleach, The Old Prison was built in the late 18th century as a 'house of correction' by the philanthropist and prison reformer, Sir George Onesiphorus Paul. He was a member of a prosperous family of Huguenot clothiers from Woodchester, who built Highgrove House, the present country home of the Prince of Wales.

The long and narrow building now houses the headquarters of the Cotswold Conservation Board, which is responsible for maintaining the Cotswold Area of Outstanding Natural Beauty. There's also a decent café and the prison section has displays in the old cells on the history of crime and punishment in Gloucestershire.

You can park at The Old Prison and walk into town along West End, a delightful curving street with a variety of silvery limestone façades, some overhung, others half timbered, but all packed with interest. Parking in the town is free.

Northleach

Overhung houses in West End

During the Battle of Britain in 1940, RAF pilots of No. 87 Squadron were billeted in Walton House, a large old coaching inn in High Street. They flew Hurricane fighter aircraft from a landing strip located between Northleach and Bibury.

At one time Walton House was a training stable and is said to be named after a descendant of a horse that won the Derby in 1787.

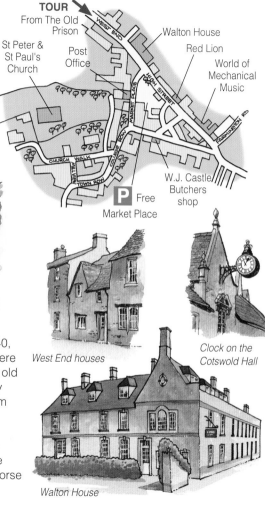

TOUR
From The Old Prison

St Peter & St Paul's Church

Post Office

Walton House

Red Lion

World of Mechanical Music

WEST END

HIGH STREET

MARKET PLACE

COLLEGE ROW

CHURCH WALK

MILL END

TOWN ROW

FARMINGTON RD

P Free
Market Place

W.J. Castle Butchers shop

West End houses

Clock on the Cotswold Hall

Walton House

106

One of the most important of all the Cotswold wool towns, Northleach was founded in the 13th century at a commercially strategic point on the crossroads of the Fosse Way and the main road from Oxford to Gloucester, midway between Cirencester and Stow-on-the-Wold. For many years heavy traffic thundered through the narrow streets but the town is now bypassed by the A40.

Northleach has suffered many ups and downs. It was hugely prosperous during the 15th century but suffered when the wool market declined. During the 18th century, coaching inns were established along High Street to cater for the growing coach trade. Some have survived, adapting to modern requirements. With the growth of the railways, coaches disappeared, but as car ownership increased, the town again became a popular refreshment stop for travellers.

High Street & Market Place

The town centre, Market Place, is compact and relatively unspoiled, having changed little since 1500, except for more 'recent' additions of late 16th and 17th-century buildings, that are split apart to form The Green.

Leave Market Place along the narrow alleys to discover houses whose upper levels of timber framing overhang great stone built walls and wide oak doors.

Most shops are owned by independent proprietors. You can buy fresh bread and cakes, newspapers and magazines, specialist wines, fine quality meats and cheese, dolls houses and furniture, music boxes, and much more.

War memorial in Market Place

W.J. Castle's butchers shop

Dubbed the 'Cathedral of the Cotswolds', the Church of St Peter and St Paul is so magnificent it's dedicated to two saints. The church was almost entirely rebuilt in the 15th century from the profits of the wool trade.

It's a splendid example of the Perpendicular style with a huge tower and a much-admired, ornate south porch decorated with a collection of finely carved corbel heads.

The interior is also lavish and beautifully proportioned, enhanced by the huge window over the chancel arch known as the *Cotswold Window*. It was the work of John Fortey and his kinsman, Thomas Fortey. Between them, the Forteys funded work which raised the nave, added the clerestory and aisles, and raised the roof. The result is a wonderfully light and open church, enriching the carving and fine architectural detail.

The church's treasures include a 15th-century goblet-shaped pulpit and a unique series of monumental brasses set in the floor which celebrate the great wool merchants of Northleach. The Cotswold wool men were powerful during the Middle Ages, not only in England but throughout Europe.

A more recent addition is new seating, designed by the Scottish architect, Sir Basil Spence and made in the furniture workshops of Gordon Russell at Broadway.

Take a stroll along Church Walk where the view of the church on the hill is sensational.

St Peter & St Paul's Church

Keith Harding's World of Mechanical Music is an unusual exhibition spread through Oak House on High Street. An eclectic mix of mechanical and musical marvels from days gone by, it features a unique collection of instruments that play themselves, from music boxes to automata. You can visit the restoration workshop and purchase clocks and musical instruments from the ever-changing collection in the shop.

Sherborne Arms

Red Lion & congregational chapel

Sadly, the still picturesque Red Lion, a former 15th-century coaching inn opposite Market Place closed in 2015.

The impressive congregational chapel next door also shares a checkered history. It was built in 1851 when the congregation numbered some 80 members, but by 1900 membership had dwindled to 28. In 1964 the chapel was in need of extensive repairs so it was sold and converted to a private house.

Market Square has been the location for several TV programmes and films, including the BBC's adaptation of J. K. Rowling's *The Casual Vacancy*. In 2002, *The Gathering* was shot here, taking over the entire market place with a fair and fake bomb explosion, and in 2015 it was again transformed, this time to look like an apocalyptic version of a Suffolk village for Sky One's mini-series *You, Me and the Apocalypse*. A video by the now deceased American singer and rapper Lil Peep was partly filmed in Northleach, and has garnered over 100 million views on YouTube.

The town sign

Food & Drink

The Black Cat Café on Market Square is community run, where you can buy simple meals and delicious cakes as well as coffee, tea and other hot drinks. Clean, cosy and good service.

Nearby, **Muzzy's Kebab & Pizza** is a friendly, fairly standard takeaway – with chips!

The **Sherborne Arms** serves value-for-money pub grub, with great atmosphere.

The **Curious Wine Cellar** is an upmarket wine bar and restaurant in an old building with a stylish modern interior, plus a private courtyard for parties. Highly-rated and curiously-named.

For the full *Country Life* experience, head for the **Wheatsheaf** in West End. A traditional British inn clad in virginia creeper, it boasts 14 uniquely-designed bedrooms, stunning tiered gardens and two private dining rooms serving locally-sourced rustic food. Dog friendly – especially labradors.

The Birdlip Round · 26 miles

Birdlip – Foston's Ash – Whiteway – Miserden – Sapperton – Waterlane – Bisley – Slad – Painswick – Sheepscombe – Foston's Ash – Birdlip

This tour is a heady mix of wide, open uplands and deep wooded valleys, best undertaken on a dry, bright day.

From Birdlip a leisurely rural drive takes us through unspoilt countryside to the laid-back village of Miserden. We then sink into rich woodland to cross the River Frome and climb steeply to elevated Jackbarrow Road. This slopes down to leafy Sapperton where we recross the Frome.

A narrow country lane then takes us to the lovely hillside village of Bisley. We continue through elevated farmland until the lane suddenly dips down a wooded hillside, twisting and turning through the hills before crossing the Painswick Stream and climbing again to Slad and the architectural gem of Painswick.

Leaving the A46 beyond the town, the route turns east to join a lane into hidden-away Sheepscombe with its celebrated restaurant and steep hills. After a final climb out of the valley we rejoin the B4070 for a restful drive back to Birdlip.

VILLAGE INNS

❶ Royal George Hotel, Birdlip
❷ Foston's Ash Inn
❸ Carpenter's Arms, Miserden
❹ The Bell, Sapperton
❺ Daneway Inn, Sapperton
❻ Stirrup Cup, Bisley
❼ Bear Inn, Bisley
❽ Woolpack, Slad
❾ Butchers Arms, Sheepscombe

ATTRACTION & CAFÉ

❿ Miserden Park Gardens

The Tour

Begin at the Royal George Hotel in Birdlip. Head west on the B4070 bearing left signed Stroud. After around 2¼ miles arrive at Foston's Ash Inn. Just beyond the inn take the left fork signed Whiteway & Miserden and at the next fork go left again signed Miserden. Go through the modest hamlet of Whiteway and at the next fork bear left signed Miserden Village only.

Royal George Hotel

Birdlip was once on the main road between Gloucester and Cirencester, now the A417. The building of a bypass, which opened in December 1988, moved the main route away from the village. A small church in the village was built in 1957, replacing one that was destroyed by fire in 1897.

Whiteway was founded in 1898 by a group of idealists who wished to follow the principles of the writer Tolstoy, sharing land, resources and much else.

Over the years their ideals were modified and the hill farm they had bought was divided into self-contained houses or bungalows. The community still exists and several of its early founders are buried in Miserden churchyard.

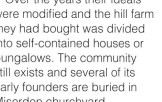

Foston's Ash Inn

❶ Royal George Hotel

Hotel restaurant serves a hearty selection of pub classics, including sizzling steaks, succulent burgers and lighter bites.

Food: 8am-10pm every day
Bar: 11am-11pm
Tel: 01452 862506
www.greenekinginns.co.uk

❷ Foston's Ash Inn

This popular free house has a reputation for great food and cosy bonhomie. All dishes are freshly made using only the finest ingredients from local suppliers. Extensive gardens with play area in the summer and open log fires in the winter. Horses, dogs and walkers welcome.

Food: Mon-Fri 11am-9pm
Sat: noon-9pm Sun: noon-8.30pm
Bar: 11am-11pm
Tel: 01452 863262
www.fostonsash.co.uk

The minute hamlet of Fostons Ash is little more than the roadside inn that's believed to be named after a former turnpike keeper. The B4070 was originally the Calf Way, a Roman road between Birdlip and Stroud.

Village centre

Miserden

Tidy, unspoilt and sometimes windy, Miserden is poised 850ft above the valley of the River Frome, near its source. The village is part of the 850-acre Miserden Estate. At its centre, outside the Carpenter's Arms, a magnificent sycamore tree shades a circular seat from where you can admire the woods of Miserden Park, the seat of the Sandys family in Elizabethan times.

This is a thriving community with a church, pub, village hall, primary school and a post office. There's a local cricket club and various groups meet regularly in the village hall. Miserden Stores, established more than a century ago, is a well-stocked convenience store and post office, open daily. A biomass boiler heats all 38 houses in the village, fuelled entirely by wood from the estate.

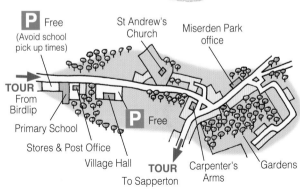

St Andrew's Church

❸ Carpenter's Arms

Very much part of the community. Serves afternoon teas all day. Good solid pub grub with ingredients sourced from the village and the local area.

Food: Mon-Sat 9am-9pm Sun 9am- 6pm
Bar: Mon-Sat 11am-11pm Sun noon-10.30pm
Tel: 01285 821283
www.thecarps-miserden.co.uk

❿ Miserden Park Gardens

Terraces overlooking the Golden Valley with fine topiary, some designed by Edwin Lutyens. Walled garden and a Parterre with a sundial at its centre. An octagonal summerhouse was built in 1999 to mark the Millennium, with an ornate fountain. Car park. Café serves refreshments and snacks. Open when the park is.

Garden open: Jan & Feb weekends 10am-5pm. Mar-Dec Tue-Sun 10am-5pm
Admission charge
Tel:01285 821303
www.miserden.org

St Andrew's parish church has Saxon origins but was drastically altered in a 19th-century restoration. However, it does contain some magnificent monuments, including effigies of Sir William Sandys and his wife, Margaret Culpepper, dressed in elaborate Stuart costumes and meticulously carved in Derbyshire alabaster. A painted effigy of William Kingston (died 1614) has him resting his feet on a goat which is complacently eating a cabbage. No one knows why.

The war memorial across the road was designed by Sir Edwin Lutyens, who was also responsible for a new wing on the house in Miserden Park and some reshaping of the garden.

Carpenter's Arms

Leave Miserden on the road past the Carpenter's Arms. At a junction of a number of roads turn left signed Edgeworth 1½. At the second turning, signed Edgeworth, turn left into a narrow, wooded road twisting downhill to cross the River Frome. Climb up the eastern side of the valley to a T-junction (Jackbarrow Road) and turn right signed Sapperton 3 and Stroud 10½. Turn right at the next junction, signed Sapperton ½, where a narrow road leads to the Bell and the upper village.

Sapperton

Dramatically set on a hillside high above the wooded Frome Valley, Sapperton enjoys spectacular views, especially when the woods are ablaze with autumn colours.

Beyond the Bell the road takes a sharp left turn where there's a small car park. The church is down a steep pathway on your right.

The road continues down an attractive sloping terrace into the valley. Sapperton was part of the late 19th-century Arts and Crafts Movement and its leading lights designed many of the buildings at the east end of the village.

St Kenelm's Church

A largely 18th-century building with an attractive broached tower, St Kenelm's Church snuggles comfortably into the wooded hillside. The stylish interior utilised much Jacobean woodwork brought from Sapperton Manor after the death of Sir Robert Atkyns in 1711. The house was demolished around 1730. There are two fine monuments in the church, both with life-sized figures. One is to Sir Henry Poole and his family, the other to Sir Robert Atkyns, the noted Gloucestershire historian and local Member of Parliament. Poole, a landowner and politician (died 1616), left money in his will for the erection of a 'comely and convenient tomb'.

❹ The Bell

Multi award-winning pub with roaring log fires in winter and a landscaped garden and courtyard in summer. Famous for its hearty traditional food prepared with fresh ingredients, well-priced and served with a smile. Included in *The Times Top Places to Eat* in 2018 after journalist Giles Coren dined here. Children and horses are also welcome.

Open: Tue-Sat 11am-11pm Sun noon-9pm
Food served: Tue-Thu noon-2.30pm & 6-9pm Fri noon-2.30 & 6-9.30pm Sat noon-2.30pm & 6-9.30pm Sun noon-4pm
Tel: 01285 760298
www.bellsapperton.co.uk

The Bell

Continue on the road through Sapperton to a green at crossroads on the edge of the village. Go straight across signed Edgeworth 2¼ and Bisley 3½. Cross the River Frome to the Daneway Inn.

The Daneway Inn was originally three cottages built in 1784 to accommodate workers

Daneway Inn

building the nearby Sapperton Tunnel. When it was finished the cottages were converted into a pub, appropriately called the Bricklayer's Arms. It became the Daneway in the 1950s when it was owned by a wealthy Stroud bookmaker who owned a racehorse named Daneway. When it won a race he had the sign repainted in its honour. The inn overlooks the canal but some of it has been filled in to make room for the car park.

The ornate Coates portal

Sapperton Canal goes through a tunnel beneath the village, emerging at its north-western end at Daneway. The tunnel was opened in 1789 on the Thames and Severn Canal after five years of construction, mostly digging through solid rock. It's over two miles long and has no tow path.

The canal was superseded by the arrival of the railway and fell into decay during the 1920s. There's a public house at each end, the Tunnel House, near the Coates portal in the centre of Hailey Wood, and the Daneway Inn at the other.

❺ Daneway Inn

A secluded and well-regarded pub with locally sourced, homemade food, well-kept ales and a friendly welcome. Converted from three 18th-century cottages, it's a warren of nooks and crannies with cosy fireplaces set against fresh white cottage walls and surrounded by a miscellany of tables and furnishings. The Thames and Severn canal runs through its garden and the valley location is a haven for wildlife.

Open: Mon-Sun noon-11pm
Food served: Mon-Sat noon-9pm
Sun noon-4pm & 5.30-9pm
Tel: 01285 760297
www.thedaneway.pub

Continue into the single track road opposite the pub signed Waterlane 1½ and Bisley 3. Cross Holy Brook and climb through woodland to a more open aspect as the road twists into the pretty little settlement of Waterlane. Keep straight on ignoring a sign indicating Bisley 1½ and Stroud 5. At about 1¼ miles beyond Waterlane you arrive at a T-junction and turn right signed The Camp 2½ and Stroud 4. Enter Bisley at the Stirrup Cup Inn and turn sharp left into the narrow main street.

Bisley

A large but compact village sitting at the head of a combe high on the wolds overlooking the Golden Valley of the River Frome. Bisley emjoys a wonderful setting and has a striking mix of fine Cotswold architecture in the well-kept cottages and large houses with colourful gardens.

Bisley is a typical example of the steep hill villages near Stroud. Row upon row of stone houses rise each side of the long and narrow High Street like an impressive ampitheatre. The street is too narrow for tourist coaches and it's difficult to park a car – even for residents – without getting in someone's way. There are no front gardens and the houses are flush with the pavement. You may be able to park on the wider road near one of the two pubs.

Narrow High Street

The village grew with the Cotswold wool trade and later there was work in the textile mills along the Frome. The clothier's wealth built many fine houses and cottages in the village, but during the mid-19th century the area suffered great poverty. Bisley survived and is now largely a peaceful commuter village for Stroud.

There's much to enjoy in long High Street and some wonderful surprises. The famous Bisley Wells are at the bottom where five springs issue from an elegant stone semicircle and two others flow into stone cattle troughs.

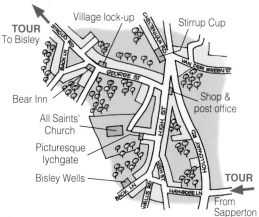

TOUR
To Bisley

Village lock-up
Stirrup Cup
STROUD RD
CHELTENHAM RD
VAN DER BREEN ST
GEORGE ST
Bear Inn
Shop & post office
All Saints' Church
HIGH ST
Picturesque lychgate
HOLLOWTN RD
BISLEY RD
Bisley Wells
BACK LN
WELLS RD
HAYHEDGE LN
TOUR
From Sapperton

❻ Stirrup Cup

Traditional 19th-century inn and restaurant serving well-kept ales and home-cooked food. Very much the village pub to pop in for a pint and a game of darts with the locals. **Open: Mon & Tue 6-9pm Wed & Thu noon-3pm & 6-11pm Fri & Sat noon-11.30pm Sun noon-10.30pm Food served: Tue 6.30-8.30pm Wed-Sat noon-2pm & 6.30-9pm Sun noon-3pm Tel: 01452 770007 www.thestirrupcup.com**

❼ Bear Inn

Of 17th-century origins and the oldest pub in Bisley, the Bear has a picturesque exterior with an appealing contemporary style inside, plus a friendly atmosphere much loved by locals and visitors. Great modern food served seven days a week with a wide range of ales, fine wines, lagers and soft drinks. One superior B&B room.

Open: Mon-Thu noon-3pm & 6-11pm Tue 6-9pm Wed & Thu noon-3pm & 6-11pm Fri noon-3pm & 6pm-12am Sat noon-2pm & 6pm-12am Sun noon-10.30pm. Food served daily noon-9pm Tel: 01452 770265 www.thebisleybear.co.uk

Stirrup Cup

Bear Inn and village lock-up

All Saints' Church boasts an impressive spire but the interior is stark, yet another example of over-zealous Victorian restoration.

However, there is an effigy of a 13th-century knight and a font with a Norman bowl set upon a 19th-century stem plus a picturesque lychgate. Seek out the Poor Soul's Light in the churchyard, a 13th-century stone structure thought to have held candles for masses to be said for the redemption of the souls of the poor. It's believed to be the only outdoor example of its kind in England.

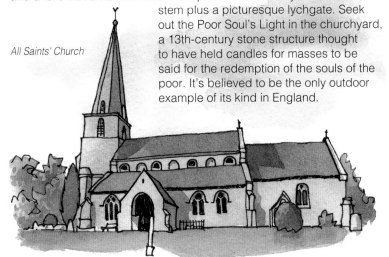

All Saints' Church

The Bear Inn at the top of George Street has 17th-century columns supporting the upper floor. At one time it was owned by one of Nelson's captains and has a 58ft well in the cellar, plus a mysterious tunnel going towards the church. The inn was probably the old court house, as the 19th-century two person village lock-up is nearby. Restored in 1998, it has two cells open to the elements – and no facilities.

Leave Bisley on Stroud Road past the Bear Inn into a wide aspect with panoramic views across wooded countryside. Soon after the road swings left at a small triangular-shaped green, turn right into a narrow unclassified road signed Ansteads Farm & Catswood (Catswood Lane). Pass the fine gateway to Ansteads Farm.

The route now becomes more challenging as the lane narrows and drops into the valley, twisting and turning through woodland with sensational views as you clear the trees. Go through Elcombe, a picturesque hamlet of lightly coloured Cotswold stone houses stacked up the wooded hillside.

Continue into Knapp Lane which contours around Swift's Hill, a wildlife reservation with an excellent viewpoint from the top. Pass Knapp Farm and at a T-junction keep straight on. Cross Slad Brook at a handful of smart houses and climb a steep hill. At the top turn sharp right (unsigned) onto the A4070 . Continue to the hamlet of Slad, from where you can admire the view across the valley that you have just negotiated.

Elcombe

Holy Trinity Church

Slad

It's attractive enough but has only a sprinkling of houses along the A4070 and few visitors would travel to Slad if it wasn't for the iconic Woolpack Inn and the legacy of author Laurie Lee.

His most famous work *Cider with Rosie*, a lyrical portrait of his early childhood in the village, has become an enduring classic selling more than six million copies since it was first published in 1959 and never been out of print. The cottage where his family lived sits by a lake in the bottom of the valley, now a private house and not open to the public.

Lee left Slad when he was twenty to work in London but went on to spend four years in Spain, becoming a volunteer in the Republican International Brigades for a while, fighting Franco's Nationalists in the Spanish Civil War. This experience provided material for the other two of his celebrated biographical trilogy.

The proceeds from *Cider with Rosie* allowed him to buy a cottage in Slad and in the 1960s he returned with his wife Catherine to live here permanently after 30 years away. Lee died in 1997 at the age of 82 and is buried in Holy Trinity churchyard. His simple headstone carries the inscription 'He lies in the valley he loved' beneath a garland of roses.

Woolpack Inn

❽ Woolpack Inn

Steeped in history and character, the Woolpack has been a public house for over 300 years and is one of the last independent gems of a British country pub. Daniel Chadwick, who part owns Lypiatt Park, one of the most beautiful and historic private estates in the region, has also owned the pub for more than 20 years.

Entering the Woolpack with its thick stone walls, small windows and outside toilets is like stepping back in time, unspoiled by passing fads and famed for its lifelong association with the poet Laurie Lee. The food is well above average too.

Open: Sun-Mon noon-11pm Tue-Thu noon-12am Fri-Sat noon-1am
Food served: Lunch Tue-Sat noon-3pm
Dinner Mon-Sat 6-9pm
Sunday lunch noon-4pm
Tel: 01452 813429
www.thewoolpackslad.com

A steep climb up the hillside from the Woolpack leads to Holy Trinity Church, built in 1831 by Charles Baker of Painswick, which looks pretty outside but has a rather plain interior. A gallery, added in 1836, was removed in 1869 when a north aisle and porch were added, designed by Benjamin Bucknall. A stained glass window commemorates Laurie Lee and a permanent display celebrates his life and the history of the church.

The single-story village schoolroom snuggles up against the steep bank opposite the Woolpack. Laurie Lee must have sat at his wooden desk with a china inkwell gazing through the mullioned windows at the inn where he spent so much of his later life and yet never mentions it in any of his books. Now you can sit in Lee's seat in the pub and gaze through the window at his old school – which he must have often done himself.

Continue on the A4070 for about a mile then turn left at Bulls Cross, (once a notorious spot for highwaymen – and a gibbet!) signed 'Painswick light vehicles only' (Greenhouse Lane). Where the road forks, take the right-hand lane down a steep (1:7) hill to cross the Painswick Stream. Climb to join Tibbiwell Lane, one of the grandest entrances into Painswick.

The Golden Heart Inn has long gone but its beautiful wrought iron sign remains

Tibbiwell

Parking in the narrow streets of central Painswick is well-nigh impossible without causing annoyance to local residents. However, there is a handy free car park in Stroud road just beyond the churchyard.

Town or village? It's difficult to tell here. Central Painswick looks like an dignified town, but its proportions are that of a village. Stroll the half-dozen or so lanes and soak up the soothing atmosphere from the ancient stone, but don't expect to do much shopping. Painswick is long on elegant architecture but short on shops, sophisticated or otherwise.

Painswick

A small town with an intricate pattern of narrow streets and dignified 17th and 18th-century buildings of the local silver-grey stone. Painswick is serenely set on a high spur above the Painswick Stream with views across a wooded valley to Bulls Cross. It's difficult to argue with Painswick's much-quoted epithet, 'Queen of the Cotswolds'.

From a cottage industry of spinning and weaving, Painswick grew to an important cloth-making centre during the 16th century after Flemish weavers built fulling and finishing mills along the river. Huge prosperity funded the building of the town's finest buildings using stone quarried from nearby Painswick Beacon.

There's no obvious centre to Painswick. It's just a meandering maze of picturesque streets that are a delight for the visitor to explore.

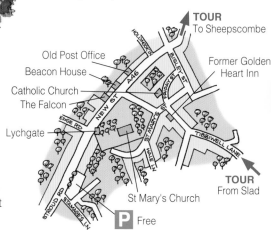

TOUR To Sheepscombe

Old Post Office
Beacon House
Catholic Church
The Falcon
Lychgate

Former Golden Heart Inn

St Mary's Church

TOUR From Slad

P Free

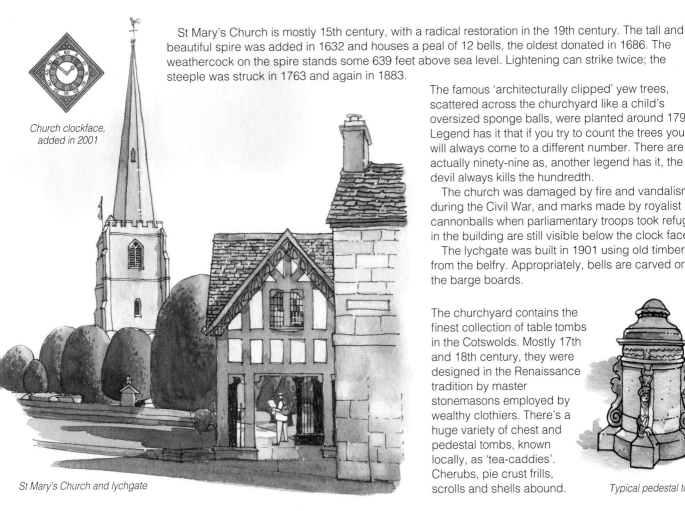

St Mary's Church is mostly 15th century, with a radical restoration in the 19th century. The tall and beautiful spire was added in 1632 and houses a peal of 12 bells, the oldest donated in 1686. The weathercock on the spire stands some 639 feet above sea level. Lightening can strike twice; the steeple was struck in 1763 and again in 1883.

The famous 'architecturally clipped' yew trees, scattered across the churchyard like a child's oversized sponge balls, were planted around 1792. Legend has it that if you try to count the trees you will always come to a different number. There are actually ninety-nine as, another legend has it, the devil always kills the hundredth.

The church was damaged by fire and vandalism during the Civil War, and marks made by royalist cannonballs when parliamentary troops took refuge in the building are still visible below the clock face.

The lychgate was built in 1901 using old timbers from the belfry. Appropriately, bells are carved on the barge boards.

The churchyard contains the finest collection of table tombs in the Cotswolds. Mostly 17th and 18th century, they were designed in the Renaissance tradition by master stonemasons employed by wealthy clothiers. There's a huge variety of chest and pedestal tombs, known locally, as 'tea-caddies'. Cherubs, pie crust frills, scrolls and shells abound.

Church clockface, added in 2001

St Mary's Church and lychgate

Typical pedestal tomb

The picturesque Old Post Office, built in 1478, still stands battered by modern traffic in New Street. Until its closure in 2003, the building was the oldest in Britain to contain a post office. It has the only exposed timber framing in the town, though many houses are timbered inside.

Our Lady & St Thérèse Roman Catholic Church in Friday Street is peaceful now after being converted from a slaughterhouse in 1934 and suffering World War II bomb damage in 1941. The pretty cupola was added in 1954-56.

Our Lady & St Thérèse Catholic Church

Town Hall doorway, Victoria Square, dated 1840

Almshouse doorway, dated 1924

The Old Post Office

Frederick Gyde was a great benefactor of the town, with a row of almshouses and an orphanage bearing his name. A street is also named in his honour.

Beacon House

Food & Drink

For coffee and cake the **Painswick Pooch** in New Street has it all, plus a library room and art exhibition. **St Michael's Restaurant** in Victoria Street and **Cardynham House Bistro** in Tiddiwell Street are smart restaurants and guest houses. For real country pub atmosphere try the **Royal Oak** in St Mary's Street, which serves real ale, cider and locally-sourced pub grub.

A 16th-century up-market hotel and restaurant, the **Falcon Inn** occupies a prime site overlooking the church in New Street.

St Mary's Street

Beacon House, in New Street opposite the church, is the epitome of Painswick elegance and sophistication. The splendid Palladian style house was built for clothier Thomas Gardner in 1604. Dynevor House, next door is dated 1801. Have a stroll down St Mary's Street, which sweeps around the churchyard and is lined with affluent Cotswold-style houses.

Almost unbelievably, narrow Bisley Street was once Painswick's main street and is still flanked by largely unaltered 14th-century façades.

Leave Painswick heading north on the A46. Half a mile out of the village turn right, signed Sheepscombe 1½ & The Butchers Arms. Descend into the valley where the road narrows to barely one car width and twists and turns through woodland to the Butchers Arms.

Butchers Arms

Sheepscombe

Set in a narrow valley hidden behind the Cotswold scarp, Sheepscombe was sparsely populated 500 years ago. The modern village developed in the 17th century on the back of agriculture and the growing textile trade. But competition and mechanisation brought a decline in the fabrics industry and the mills began to close, the last in 1839.

Sheepscombe, like most of the area, was plunged into a period of poverty and falling population. Since then the number of residents has increased and today it's a vibrant community, with a primary school, cricket club, village hall, church and a popular pub, although no longer the working village that it was. Most of its inhabitants are from the professional middle classes, who pay dearly for the privilege of living in such a beautiful place. Situated at the bottom of a steep valley, Sheepscombe is a relatively inaccessible village with only three steep and narrow lanes leading into it, so it's not easy for those without a car. Hard winters can present a huge problem.

9 Butchers Arms

Much-acclaimed village gastropub, dating from 1670. Scores highly on food, service and atmosphere. 'Gets everything right' is a typical review.

The Sheepscombe Valley was once part of a Royal Deer Park for Henry VIII and the pub name comes from the practice of hanging the carcasses of deer killed on the hunt in what is now the bar. Over the years the pub extended into the next door alehouse and two adjacent cottages. Fortunately, many of the old features such as massive fireplaces, thick stone walls and mullioned windows have been preserved.

The carved pub sign is almost as famous as the pub. Much-photographed, it depicts a butcher sipping a pint of beer with a pig tied to his leg, and has appeared in many publications on the subject.

**Open: Mon-Thu 11.30am-3pm & 6.30-11pm Fri & Sat 11.30am-11pm
Sun noon-10.30pm
Food served: Mon-Fri noon-2.30pm & 6.30-9.30pm Sat noon-9.30pm
Sun noon-6pm
Tel: 01452 812113
www.butchers-arms.co.uk**

The Church of St John the Apostle was built by the villagers and consecrated in 1820 after Agnes Neville, wife of the curate of Painswick, despaired of 'this Godless place with fourteen ale houses!'. Constructed of limestone ashlar with a stone slate roof to coped gables, it was designed by John Wight and expanded in 1872 by Francis Niblett. English Heritage has listed the church as Grade II for its special architectural and historic interest.

Built high on the southern hillside, the church is visible from all over the village, but with a dinky little tower attached to its ornate west end it's far too pretty to strike fear into any hardened drinker.

Church of St John the Apostle

Cottages on the southern slopes

The school was opened in 1822, with a modernised building opening on the same site in 1882. Many of the houses at the northern side of the village date from the late 17th and early 18th centuries.

Though criss-crossed by narrow lanes, Sheepscombe is spread quite thinly so there's several places where you can park without inconveniencing anybody.

Continue along the narrow road through Sheepscombe. Cross the Painswick Stream and, after climbing steeply to the war memorial, keep straight on with the church on your right. Continue to climb to a bend from where there's a great view across the village. Keep on climbing through woodland, turning left at the first junction. After about 600 yards join the B4070, turning left for the 3½ miles or so back to Birdlip, where this tour ends.

Author's Notes

The Cotswolds

The area lies on a band of oolite limestone arcing across England from Dorset to the Humber where the land has tilted up on its western side to form an escarpment with a gentle slope to the east. Designated 'An Area of Outstanding Natural Beauty' (AONB), the largest in England and Wales, the Cotswolds stretch 80 miles from Chipping Campden in the north, to Bath in the south, covering an area of 790 sq. miles, 80 per cent of which is farmland. It has the largest number of conservation areas of any region and has been shaped by people for over 6,000 years. The AONB has over 3,000 miles of public footpaths. Around 85,000 people live in the Cotswolds, one of the lowest population densities in England, with fewer than 300 residents in over half its parishes. Attracting some 38 million day visitors a year, the region's principle industry is tourism, generating over £130 million a year.

Cotswold stone

The Cotswolds are rich in oolitic limestone and so it was natural to start building with it in the Middle Ages due to its availability and comparative cheapness. There are still quarries in the region extracting and working the stone for repairs and the construction of new buildings. The old limestone houses and cottages are invariably 'listed' buildings, which means they are strictly protected from alteration. The colour of the stone depends on where it was quarried. Generally, in the northern part of the Cotswolds the stone is honey golden brown and further south it becomes more silvery in colour.

J.B. Priestley wrote of Cotswold stone: 'Even when the sun is obscured and the light is cold, these walls are still faintly warm and luminous, as if they knew the trick

Painswick doorway

of keeping the lost sunlight of centuries glimmering about them.'

The Cotswold Way

A long distance footpath between Chipping Campden in the north and Bath in the south. 102 miles in length, It runs through prime Cotswold countryside along the escarpment and is well-marked and maintained. There are many other fine walks in the region

Fosse Way

A Roman road running through the Cotswolds, so called from the fosse or ditch that used to run along each side. It linked Exeter, in south-west England, with Lincoln in the East Midlands, and is now the A429.

Morris Dancing

Practiced in many parts of England but most commonly in the Cotswolds, Morris dancing is a folk dance performed outdoors – usually not far from a pub – by men wearing costumes consisting of a white shirt and trousers, and a hat adorned with flowers and ribbon. Garters are worn around the legs with bells attached. Handkerchiefs or sticks are used in the dance and a fiddle or concertina provides the music. The dance often illustrates a legend or a rural activity such as sowing and harvesting, with the bells and handkerchiefs warding off evil spirits to ensure the fertility of the crops for the coming year.

Sheep

In the Middle Ages (5th to 15th centuries) the Cotswolds were well-known throughout Europe as the source of some of the best wool. The high wolds were ideal for

Royalist Hotel, Stow-on-the-Wold

grazing sheep and the abbeys and monasteries raised huge flocks of the 'Cotswold Lions'. These native sheep were large animals with long, golden fleeces. Wool merchants became enormously rich and spent much of their wealth on lavish church restoration, as well as building fine houses for themselves. In the Middle Ages 50 per cent of England's economy was based on wool.

Source of the River Thames
Most experts agree that the source of the Thames is in the Cotswolds but the precise location is a matter of hot debate. The traditional source is at Thames Head, north of Cirencester. It's a spring that only flows intermittently so there's also strong claims for Seven Springs, further north near Cheltenham, where the River Churn also rises. The alternative source would add another 14 miles to the river's 'official' 215-mile length.

Stone walls
The first great wall-building period in the Cotswolds was during the 18th century with the land enclosures. The second came in the 19th century when the land-owners built walls around their estates. The walls are usually about two feet wide at the bottom and narrow to around fourteen inches at the top. The middle is filled with rubble and every so often a 'bonder' is put in as a strengthener and can be left sticking out to make a stile. At the required height, rows of stones are set upright to complete the wall. No cement or earth is used so air can permeate and the

construction remains dry. A properly built wall will last many hundreds of years with relatively little maintenance.

Thames & Severn Valley Canal
The canal was opened in 1789, linking the Stroudwater Canal at Stroud with the head of the navigable Thames at Lechgate, through the Sapperton Tunnel (see page 115). There were problems with leakage and an abnormal number of locks, but the canal's fate was sealed when the Great Western Railway was opened in 1845. The company bought the canal and stopped all traffic on it, allowing the waterway to become derelict. Its closure was one of the great tragedies of English canal history and although efforts have been made to reopen some sections, it's difficult to believe that this outstandingly beautiful link between two great river systems will ever be reopened in its entirety.

Town or village?
When one becomes the other is a matter for debate. As a rough rule of thumb, towns have market squares and villages have greens.

House at Little Barrington

Vernacular architecture
The Cotswolds building style is justifiably famous. It includes the use of local limestone in the walls and roof; a steeply pitched roof (60 degrees) usually with dormers; ridge tiles and coping; tall chimneys; large window sills of stone or wood; and detailed window mouldings of stone.

Some English History

The English Reformation
Part of a general discontent with the power of the Holy Roman Empire throughout Europe during the 16th century, the English reformation centred on Henry VIII's struggle with the Pope to have his marriage to Catherine of Aragon annulled so that he could marry his pregnant mistress, Anne Boleyn. The matter was resolved in 1533, when Thomas Cranmer, appointed Archbishop of Canterbury by the king, annulled the marriage and Catherine was forbidden to appeal to Rome. In 1534, on the King's instructions, parliament passed the Act of Supremacy, declaring him to be the Supreme Head of the English Church.

The Dissolution of the Monasteries (1536-40)
To complete the break with Rome, Henry VIII disbanded some 825 religious communities throughout England, Wales and Ireland. Abbeys, monasteries, priories, convents and friaries were destroyed and monastic land, around a third of all parishes, was seized by the Crown and quickly sold on, usually to the local gentry and nobility. The Dissolution is still the largest 'legal' transfer of property in English history since the Norman Conquest. It had a profound effect on the Cotswolds region which persists to this day.

The English Civil Wars (1642-49)
A series of armed conflicts between royalist supporters of King Charles I (Cavaliers) and the parliamentarians (Roundheads). The Cotswolds, a royalist-leaning region, became a battleground when the king set up his headquarters at Oxford. The wars ended with the trial and execution of Charles I in 1649 and the establishment of a republic led by Oliver Cromwell.